KU-077-789

CONTENTS

'People who try to pretend they're superior make it so much harder for those of us who really are.'

Hyacinth Bucket
Keeping Up Appearances

THE *Bluffer's*® GUIDE TO

ETIQUETTE

William Hanson

Hammersley House
5-8 Warwick Street
London W1B 5LX
United Kingdom

Email: info@bluffers.com
Website: bluffers.com
Twitter: @BluffersGuide

First published 2014
First reprint 2015
Copyright © Bluffer's® 2014

Publisher: Thomas Drewry
Publishing Director: Brooke McDonald

Series Editor: David Allsop
Design and Illustration: Jim Shannon

ISBN: 978-1-909937-00-0 (print)
      978-1-909937-01-7 (ePub)
      978-1-909937-02-4 (Kindle)

TO THE MANNERS BORN

Etiquette is a product of France, which comes as a great annoyance to the British who would like to be able to claim its invention as their own. Louis XIV (1638-1715), the foppish 'Sun King', decided to come up with little 'tickets' to place around his palace at Versailles for his courtiers to observe. 'Keep off the grass' (or, more correctly, '*défense de marcher sur le gazon*') is widely thought to have been the very first of these tickets, as Versailles did – and still does – have lovely lawns that would be spoiled by clodhopping *paysans* tramping all over them.

The irony is that the country which largely eliminated its upper classes in the revolution of 1789 has to a great extent written the lexicon of etiquette. You will therefore need to possess an easy familiarity with such words and expressions as *lèse-majesté, noblesse oblige, politesse, place à table, de rigueur…* All will become clear in due course.

You must also be aware that manners and etiquette are more or less the same thing; do not even begin to suggest otherwise. They are most certainly bedfellows; manners need etiquette to survive and vice versa. Manners are the guiding principles of respect and social interaction, and etiquette is the unwritten code of exact rules. Such as with football – the aim is to score a goal, and things like the offside rule help you to fairly and correctly score that goal*. Apparently.

Some may think that in the über-progressive second decade of the twenty-first century (there is no hard and fast rule about how to describe this period, but please don't say 'teenies'), etiquette would have died a death. *Au contraire!* In Britain we are now even more obsessed by social codes and *politesse* than ever before. You may be more Crystal Palace than Buckingham Palace, but with the right knowledge you will go far. Families like the Middletons are prime examples.

But, like them and the rest of us, there are occasions when you will have to bluff. And here you enter perilous territory, which is where this short guide can offer invaluable help. It sets out to conduct you through the main danger zones encountered in discussions about etiquette in British society, and to equip you with a vocabulary and evasive technique that will minimise the risk of being rumbled as a bluffer. It will give you a few easy-to-learn hints and methods that might even allow you to be accepted as an etiquette expert of rare ability and experience. But it will do more. It will give you the tools to impress legions of marvelling listeners with your knowledge and insight – without anyone discovering that, until you read it, you probably didn't know the difference between *comme il faut* and a *faux pas*.

*The author cannot take this analogy further as – and this may come as a shock – he does not care for the sport.

HOW DO YOU DON'T

GREETINGS AND SMALL TALK

Men in white coats have concluded that we judge someone within the first three to six seconds of meeting them. Those who go around making bold proclamations like 'I don't care what people think of me' are lying (and not doing a good job of hiding it). Of course they care. We all do. As the old cliché tells us, 'we only have one chance to make a first impression'. Everything, from what we wear, to how we look, to what we say, counts.

But let us begin by focusing on what should (and should not) emanate from the mouth if the bluffer wants to be accepted as a member of polite society.

Do say 'How do you do?'

Don't say 'Pleased to meet you.'

'How do you do?' is a rhetorical question and those who answer it will have fallen at the first hurdle. Instead, repeat it back at your interlocutor, together with your name. Thus, the ideal greeting will go like this:

Mr Smith 'Good morning, how do you do? John Smith.'

Mr Jones 'George Jones, how do you do?'

'Pleased to meet you' should be avoided for two reasons. The first is that if you have never met them before, you do not know if you are pleased to meet them or not, and we can leave this sort of treacly insincerity to the Americans, who are all having nice days. Second, among certain social strata, 'pleased (or nice) to meet you' is treated as rather suspect. When the Middleton family first entered into Prince William's life, his peers apparently referred to them as the 'Nice-to-meet-you Middletons'.*

'I'm so glad to meet you at last', or words to that effect, is acceptable when meeting someone with whom you may have exchanged emails, telephone conversations, tweets and the like. In that instance, 'How do you do?' may seem a bit too aloof.

THE HANDSHAKE

Although you must pick your moment, your audience will be greatly impressed if you can casually drop into conversation the origins and reasoning behind the

---

*Apropos any discussion involving this perfectly nice and respectable middle-class family, the correct position to take is to say: 'There is a difference between snobbery and etiquette. While both may be wielded as a social weapon, the former is really very bad form – rather like stabbing someone with your left hand while shaking with your right.' See 'The Handshake'.

handshake. We all shake hands frequently, but surprisingly few people realise why.

Historically, gentlemen would frequently carry swords as you could never be quite sure who your friends were. When about to engage in combat they would unsheathe their weapons using their right hand, as the sword was carried in a scabbard on their left hip. When meeting someone who was 'a friend' they would show that they meant them no harm by presenting their right hand, away from the left hip, palm open – to confirm they were not holding a weapon. The fact that some frightful cads then produced a dagger in their left hand and stabbed their unsuspecting 'friend' is a minor detail you can leave out.

So that's the history sorted, but you need to back up your knowledge with a good shake yourself. It's the only skin-on-skin contact you will (probably) have with that person, and many will judge others on the quality of their wrist action:

Use your right hand, even if you are left-handed. You only shake with the left hand in the Scouts – or if you have no right hand (in these circumstances the bluffer must improvise).

Make eye contact. No need to stare, but avoiding eye contact implies nervousness or dishonesty; even if you do feel nervous because you're meeting a social superior, don't show it. This is early bluffing territory in the world of etiquette. Keep them guessing.

Shake once or twice. In China, the handshake will go on for much longer – in fact, so long that wrists have been known to get sprained. But in Britain we just get it over and done with as quickly as possible.

Strength of grip is important. Knuckle-crunching impresses nobody and smacks of trying too hard. Soft, moist and limp conveys timidity. Aim for somewhere in between.

Smile! Nothing is more certain to make a good impression than a good smile. Again, don't go overboard by doing a hideous impersonation of Tony Blair; just smile quite naturally.

THE SOCIAL KISS

Today the social kiss is pandemic. You can't move at a party for any old Tom, Dick or Harry wanting to come up to kiss you. Traditionally, the British are very reserved about these things and are reluctant to show much, or indeed any, emotion to those they do not know very, very well. Typically, they only show affection to dogs or horses.

If you lean in to kiss someone upon first greeting, or even on first departure since meeting them, then your cards will be marked. Not that the kissee will say or do anything at the time – good manners dictate that they will behave as if it was perfectly natural.

You should only kiss once, unless you are of a particularly artistic nature or have worked in the theatre, where a two-kiss greeting is the norm. With the increase and ease of travel, some pasty Brits have begun to fancy themselves as continental *boulevardiers* and are kissing twice now, for no apparent reason. In some parts of France – and in the Netherlands, too – they kiss not once, not twice, but thrice! Thankfully this is yet to penetrate British kissing culture to any significant extent. Except in the environs of Sloane Square.

♛

'The important thing is not what they think of me, but what I think of them.'

Queen Victoria

Chaps should take the lead from the girls. If the girl proffers her cheek then he may go in for the social kiss. If a hand is offered, then no kissing is likely to occur.

A social kiss involves no lips or silly sound effects. One cheek is pressed gently against the other, and that is that. If you aim for the lips don't be surprised to find yourself kissing an ear on a swiftly swivelled head.

Some elderly ladies may offer you a downturned hand, which is a sign that you are beyond a handshake, but not quite at a social kiss.

Don't kiss the actual hand with your lips – especially if you have a tendency to leave a residue of saliva.

Do bow slightly to the hand, bringing it two inches away from your lips.

SMALL TALK

After you have greeted your acquaintance, it is customary to move into the murky depths of small talk, which the British are quite good at, even if they do say so themselves. Had this been an Olympic sport back in the summer of 2012, they would have trounced the Americans and Chinese. The Germans are the worst at small talk, as they can't see the point of not getting straight to the point.

Small talk is much more than making comments about the weather. It's about summing up the conversational skills of your opponent. Do they make you laugh, cry, sad or mad? If you like what you hear then you stay; if not, you leave. The language choices you must make if you wish to cut it with the cut-glass set will be addressed later, but there are certain topics that need to be handled with care or, preferably, not at all, for good conversation:

Avoid sex, money, health, politics and religion.

Discuss how one knows the hosts, the weather, horses, if one has travelled far.

If you get stuck with a social bore, there is a polite and effective way to get rid of them. Simply find someone floundering nearby (having observed them in your keen room-scanning peripheral vision), introduce the bore to them saying 'there's someone you simply must meet', and then beat a speedy retreat citing that you must catch someone before they leave.

WHAT YOU SAY

When engaging in conversation, your language choice and vocabulary can set you apart from the hoi polloi (or put you among it) with just a few syllables. To borrow the cliché, it is a minefield. Practice will make perfect. Use the right words and you can rest assured that you'll be among the Saved when God comes to make his final judgement:

Do say	Don't say
America	The States
bag	handbag
baked potato	jacket potato
beaker	mug
comfortable	comfy
die	passed away (or any other euphemism)
dinner jacket	tuxedo
first course	starter
Good health!	Cheers!
have a bath	take a bath (you're not taking it anywhere!)
have tea	take tea
historic house	stately home
How do you do?	Pleased to meet you
lavatory	toilet
London	town (as in 'going up to town')
Mothering Sunday	Mother's Day
napkin	serviette
pudding	dessert, sweet or 'afters'

Do say	Don't say
rich	wealthy/well off
riding	horse riding
Shrove Tuesday	Pancake Day
sitting room	lounge or, worse, front room
sofa	settee, couch
Sorry?	Pardon?
upmarket	posh
vegetables	greens
writing paper	notepaper

This is what Nancy Mitford and Professor Alan SC Ross termed 'U' and 'Non-U' back in the 1950s, the former category being the Upper Classes and the latter being everyone else.

Lavatory/toilet is the most well known of these examples, with the middle classes proclaiming that loo is preferable to either. Lavatory remains top of the tree; loo is permissible, however. It is only a bathroom if it's got a bath in it and, despite what Uncle Sam et al may say, you're not really going there to have a rest, so avoid the word 'restroom'.

Too many Brits get their houses confused with hotels and call that room with the comfortable chairs 'the lounge'. It's a sitting room. That is entry-level U/Non-U stuff. The advanced student will know the difference between a sitting room and a drawing room. In the grand old houses, a drawing room means a room in which to withdraw… and you would withdraw from the sitting room. Therefore, you cannot have a drawing room without having a sitting room.

If the worst word has to be picked from that second column, it would probably be 'pardon'. The U brigade do sometimes mumble and you may well be tempted to ask them to repeat themselves…but just ask 'Sorry?' Bodice-ripper novelist Jilly Cooper once overheard her son say: 'Mummy says that "pardon" is a much worse word than "f*ck".'

The upper classes do not hold with businesses and hotels changing their names. Despite what the branding, packaging or marketing bods may want them to believe, they will resist switching to the new term:

Do say	Don't say
British Rail	Network Rail
Hyde Park Hotel	Mandarin Oriental Hyde Park
Jif	Cif
Oil of Ulay	Oil of Olay
Opal Fruits	Starburst
Yellow Pages	Yell

HOW YOU SAY IT

Then there's the question of pronunciation. In order for a social climber to reach the top, you must emulate the vocal patterns of the top brass, as well as their vocabulary choices. Correct English has the stress on the first syllable for many words. 'American English' has the stress on the second syllable. Take the word 'primarily', for example:

Do say 'PRIME-rily'

Don't say 'prime-ARILY'

The pronunciation of the letter H can also be a sticky wicket. It is pronounced 'aitch', not 'haitch' (i.e., no silly aspirated H sound). There is no question about this and even allowing other people to think otherwise is just wrong. Initialisms such as HMV and HR (which should be Personnel, anyway) can lead to social suicide if pronounced incorrectly. If ever challenged about this, the bluffer's position should not budge. There is no room for negotiation. It's pronounced 'aitch', and that is final.

You must also worry about how much enthusiasm you give certain topics. The better people always play down what the other classes would make a fuss about, such as the amputation of a limb. Only very trivial topics are enthused about.

Therefore, it is 'the most wonderful baked potato!' but it's 'rather tedious losing a leg'.

When questioned by someone (regardless of their social position) as to whether your word choice matters anymore, the skilled bluffer will affect an air of nonchalance and, with a hint of mirth, say: 'Oh no, it doesn't really matter.' This is a lie, of course. It matters a great deal. It's just not done to admit it.

NAME CALLING

Since the dawn of 'Call me Tony' – and now 'Call me Dave/Ed/Nick' – the correct form of address is perhaps seen as a little bit of an anachronism. Does it even matter what you call someone? The answer, as any bluffer on the finer points of protocol will aver, is a resounding yes. The rules are not overly tricky to learn and, once mastered, help distinguish the socially adept from the chronically inept.

DO YOU CALL HIM DAVE?

Familiarity breeds contempt, as they say, and it is always preferable – no matter what the situation – to stick to using a person's title and surname (i.e., Mr. Henderson) until further notice. Politicians no longer want to be seen as our elected representatives but as our best pals. If invited to call them by their first name, however much this upsets your stomach, one would be excused for going along with it for the sake of an easy life and in the fervent hope that they soon clear off.

In recent years, being seen to be cool has become

preferable to being correct. Skilled society bluffers will shun pretty much anything that is cool and stick to custom and courtesy.

When meeting the parents of your boy/girlfriend, for example, it is still the 'done thing' to start by calling them 'Mr and Mrs Percy' rather than 'Ralph and Jane'. Children, too, should be instructed when visiting a friend's house not to use their friend's parents' first names until invited. It is an easy way to identify good breeding.

TERMS OF ENDEARMENT

Always fun, but never appropriate in a business setting – unless you work in the 'meeja' or art world. Terms of endearment should be reserved for those for whom you actually have some genuine affection. If they ask you to stop calling them by whatever name you have used, then desist without demurral.

As with most areas of etiquette and correct form, there are preferred sobriquets you can employ when addressing someone. 'Old bean/fruit', 'dear boy/girl', 'darling', 'cabbage' (reportedly the Duke of Edinburgh's nickname for the Queen) are acceptable. 'M'love', 'duckie', 'dearie' 'treacle', and 'mate' are generally unacceptable in polite society.

THE USE OF MS

This still remains a hot etiquette potato, as some women object to taking their husband's name and becoming 'Mrs John Smith', as correct form would have it. If you are writing socially to a woman who you know adopts this position, then use the handle Ms to avoid the possibility of being lectured when you next speak to her (but quietly rest assured that you have the etiquette high-ground!) In a professional context, the use of Ms is more acceptable, especially since you may not know the women's marital status, a factor which is hardly relevant to her job. Her Majesty The Queen will not acknowledge the Ms prefix, and so all letters that go out from the royal household addressed to women are either started with Miss or Mrs. Bluffers in the world of high society should follow Her Majesty's lead.

FROM MASTER TO MISTER, MSTR TO MR

If you are writing to a male person under the age of 12, then the envelope is correctly addressed as 'Master Tommy Tinker' (or Mstr, for short). When the boy reaches his teenage years then he can be styled Mister (Mr).

Female children remain Miss until they marry and are addressed as such, even if they behave like a right Madam.

WHEN IS SOMEONE AN ESQ?

Technically, an Esquire is one rank above an untitled gentleman but since the turn of the twentieth century, the courtesy title Esq has been widely used for all gentlemen – as if to imply an element of gentility.

There are several schools of thought as to its correct usage, one being that a man cannot be termed Esq without owning land or property. Thus, if a twenty-something postgrad starts renting his first flat, he remains Mr Ben

Bland until he buys property in his own name, and becomes B Bland, Esq.

Although many scoff at the usage of Esq on envelopes in the twenty-first century, it is still socially acceptable. However a man is one or the other, never Mr B Bland, Esq.

You will gain additional bluffing points if you are aware of the differing American usage of the suffix, which is given exclusively to lawyers. Or, as they often prefer to be known, attorneys.

'He seems very nice and he's got a title.'
'Yes, I'm sure he has and it's not one
you'd use in polite society.'
Joan Simms and Kenneth Williams in Carry on
Don't Lose Your Head *(1966)*

You can beguile your friends into thinking you are a regular in the royal household by making a passing reference to British males being styled, J Smith, Esq on the envelopes of invitations to royal events, whereas foreigners get styled Mr Juan Sanchez, or even Snr Juan Sanchez, if you want to be linguistically correct and the person in question happens to be a national of a Spanish-speaking country.

Note that you should never add 'Esq' after your own name – let others do it instead.

ADDRESSING SAME-SEX COUPLES

With modern times come modern dilemmas. Gay couples should be addressed on envelopes simply as 'Mr K Julian and Mr H Sandy'. Difficulties can arise with the correct form of address for female same-sex couples. Technically, if they are not married, they remain 'Miss S Richardson and Miss A Perkins'. If they get married and one chooses to adopt the other's surname then there is a strong case for them being styled 'Mrs and Mrs Richardson'. This might well have traditionalists running for the hills, but, frankly, there are bigger problems to worry about in this day and age.

COURTESY TITLES FOR SAME-SEX SPOUSES

With same-sex marriages now legal in Britain, students of the finer points of correct form have started to ponder whether the male spouses of knights of the realm and other members of the titled classes receive a courtesy title as with heterosexual female spouses. The simple answer is no. For example, there is no such thing as Lord David Furnish, or Lord David John ... much to his probable disappointment. He remains Mr David Furnish. Similarly, Reinaldo Avila da Silva, the partner of Baron Mandelson of Foy will continue to be known as such, and sadly never 'Baroness' if/when the happy couple decide to formalise their relationship.

And what happens when broadcaster Clare Balding becomes a dame, as inevitably she will. Does her partner, fellow broadcaster Alice Arnold, become in some way ennobled if they marry? Unfortunately etiquette is not always an exact science, so there's no strict answer. All things considered however, it seems unlikely.

UNMARRIED COUPLES
Unlike with married couples, where invitations to public functions will list the husband's name first followed by the wife's, and invitations to private ones will see that order reversed, unmarried couples can pose a bit of a problem.

The usual answer, by no means perfect, is to name first whichever partner is the 'official' invitee or recipient.

HONOURS AND DEGREES AFTER A NAME
Americans are particularly fond of displaying any letters they may claim the right to append to their name, evinced for example by the use of ACE in screen credits to denote membership of the society of American Cinema Editors. Even though most people won't have a clue what these letters mean, the general idea is that they must carry a certain amount of cachet and that those entitled to use them must be be taken even more seriously.

The British prefer only to use them when required and even then can feel a tad embarrassed, even apologetic, to have them in the first place. However, if for example one were writing to a medical doctor in his or her professional capacity, then letters denoting professional qualifications might be used as a matter of course, whereas in a social context they would be more likely to be overlooked.

'Bt' or 'Bart' (short for baronet) and 'Esq', if applicable, precede all other letters after the name. Other letters follow the following order of precedence.

i. Orders and decorations conferred by the Crown (e.g., GCMG, CBE, BEM)

ii. Appointments in the following order:
Privy Councillor (PC)
Aide de Camp to the Queen (ADC)
Honorary Physician to the Queen (QHP)
Honorary Surgeon to the Queen (QHS)
Honorary Dental Surgeon to the Queen (QHDS)
Honorary Nursing Sister to the Queen (QHNS)
Honorary Chaplain to the Queen (QHC)

iii. Queen's Counsel (QC)
Justice of the Peace (JP)
Deputy Lieutenant (DL)

iv. University degrees

v. Religious orders
Medical qualifications

vi. Fellowships of learned societies
Royal Academicians and Associates
Fellowships, memberships, etc. of professional bodies
Writers to the Signet

vii. Member of Parliament (MP)

viii. Membership of one of the Armed Forces (e.g., RN, RM, regimental name or RAF)

Extra points if you learn the correct name for all of the above, which is, as every etiquette bluffer should commit to memory: 'post-nominals'.

OPENING AND CLOSING A LETTER

This was once taught in all British schools, but today the correct form for written correspondence is rarely seen or heard. Possibly for that reason, it is something that etiquette experts are frequently asked to advise upon.

Salutation	Dear Sir / Dear Madam*
Subscription	Yours faithfully,
Salutation	Dear Mr Henderson,
Subscription	Yours sincerely,
Salutation	Dear Stephen,
Subscription	Yours ever,

If you are susceptible to theatrical tendencies when writing to close friends, you could use the letters of Noël Coward as a source of inspiration for more creative and flamboyant ways to sign off missives. Some examples…

---

*No one is ever a Dear Sir/Madam. They are either a Sir or a Madam. Every effort should be made by the sender to find out the gender of the recipient. 'To whom it may concern' should only be deployed when writing to a local council department.

All love and hugs,
Your affectionate, but regal,
The quaintest of quaints,
Love, love, love,

WHAT TO DO WHEN YOU FORGET SOMEONE'S NAME AT A PARTY

Finally, in this chapter about names and correct usage, a word about the most painful of party perils – forgetting the name of the person you're talking to. There are ways to stop this from happening. Some find it helpful to repeat back the person's name very shortly afterwards in conversation. Others use mnemonics, word association or rhymes (Clare lives on a square; Giles has travelled miles). Yet the best way, reportedly popularised by Noël Coward (him again), is as follows. It is only when a third party comes to speak with you both and an introduction is required that you should deploy this...

You	'Hello, Richard! Good to see you again. May I introduce...Gosh, I'm so sorry I've forgotten your name.'
Person	'Henry'
You	'No, Henry, I meant your last name'
Person	'Smith'
You	'Thank you. Henry Smith, may I introduce Richard Saunders?'

This must be done with total conviction and courage if it is to succeed, and does rely upon the person just giving their first name. If they happen to give both of their names, under no circumstances reply with, 'I meant your middle name!' If this happens to you, and you are well aware as to what trick they are pulling, have the good manners to not say anything.

But what if you bump into Henry a few weeks later, and you've forgotten his name again? Try to prompt your memory by asking: 'When was the last time we saw each other? What were we doing?' If that doesn't work, there's always the reverse tactic of saying, 'Of course you won't remember my name…'

Finally, there's the time-tested way out of forgetting someone's name when you're in the process of introducing them to an audience. 'Ladies and gentlemen, it gives me great pleasure to introduce a man/woman…who needs no introduction.'

DINNER PARTY DECORUM

Once the bluffer has been introduced to the right sort of people, provided they have followed this guide to the letter, they can expect to be invited to dine with their new acquaintances. Yet this can open up an array of new dilemmas and opportunities to make multiple *faux pas*. Your dining etiquette needs to be top drawer in order to survive.

It is more than likely that you will be invited to dine at their house, rather than a restaurant. This is the polar opposite of China, where dining at someone's house is very rarely the norm. But high society in Britain enjoys entertaining at home.

And what a good place to start – the 'At home' card. The best households will issue these a few weeks before the desired dinner date. Less organised houses may telephone with your invitation, although you can then expect a less sophisticated evening.

A good example of such a card is as follows, with the invitee's name handwritten above:

Lady Tushingham
at Home
Friday 12th May

RSVP   *Dinner, 7.30pm*
Inglenook Court
Sussex

For posted invitations you must reply within a couple of days.

It is still correct to reply to posted invitations in the third person. For example:

Mr William Darcy thanks Lady Tushingham for her kind invitation to dinner on Friday 12th May at half past seven at Inglenook Court and regrettably cannot attend/has much pleasure in accepting.

The date of your response is then written underneath. Signing your name as well is a major gaffe and will precipitate your immediate relegation back to the third division of aspiring socialites.

ACT I: ARRIVAL AND PRE-DINNER DRINKS

Even though the invitation says 7.30pm, a polite guest will arrive 10 to 15 minutes after the stated time. A good bluffer knows not to arrive bang on time.

Upon arrival, it is polite to show up with 'something'. A bottle of wine is considered a tad middle class, not to mention presumptuous – as you are unlikely to know your hosts' taste in wine. A bottle of Champagne (Bollinger or Moët are preferred) is more appropriate, but chocolates or flowers are also a smart choice (and generally less expensive).

This business of 'hostess gifts' began in the USA in the 1930s. It wasn't until the 1950s that the practice invaded British shores, and then it was just chocolates that were brought.

A small drinks reception is the custom on arrival in smarter houses. When your hosts ask you what you'd like to drink, ask for a sherry. Good homes will always have sherry. Failing that, simply say you will have whatever is going. Don't make yourself a nuisance by asking for something difficult. Asking for a branded beer like a Corona will make your host feel uneasy for two reasons: a) they won't have any and b) they will be mentally making sure they've locked away their jewellery upstairs.

Do say 'Do you have an amontillado?'

Don't say 'Could I have a vodka and Coke?'

When you are led through to dinner, a good bluffer will ask the hostess what the *placement* is. This is the French for 'seating plan'. Yet an even better bluffer will ask whether there is any *place à table* (an even smarter French label for a seating plan). This will give you maximum bluffing points and impress even the most demanding of hostesses.

Do not expect to be seated in prime position on your first outing at a proper dinner party. The best seat in the house – for a female guest – is to the right of the host, and to the right of the hostess for a male guest. These are called 'guest of honour' seats and normally go to the most senior guests (in social rank or age). Bluff correctly and very soon this may well be your default position. In the meantime, you might well find where you're sitting courtesy of a name card above the place setting. This will be roughly three inches by one-and-a-half inches in size and will bear your name (with title, where appropriate). It will usually be written in calligraphy but there are no hard and fast rules about this – except that it should be legible.

'On the Continent people
have good food; in England people
have good table manners.'

George Mikes

Correct *place à table* will ensure boy-girl-boy-girl. And you will find that quite an old-fashioned example of etiquette, still practised by the older generations – including Her Majesty The Queen – is the custom of 'turning the table'. This is where the ladies will talk to the man on their left for the first course, and then the man on their right for the next, and switch with each new course. In the days of Jane Austen, the hostess would give a polite cough in between rounds as a signal for the ladies to turn together. Perhaps that is a little over the top for today, but make sure you speak to the people each side of you – especially if you are a man. You may have a pretty young thing on one side and an old trout on the other, but you must charm them equally. It is only good manners to do so.

ACT II: THE DINING ROOM

PLACE SETTING
When you arrive at the table, a first-time bluffer who has not yet dined in high society may be puzzled to see all the cutlery down each side of the place setting. Bluffers may have been used to the pudding cutlery being set above the plate in their own homes – but that was wrong. Very wrong. Now that you are moving up in the world you will soon

realise that those who really know what's what place said cutlery down at the side with everything else. This stems from the days when crescent-shaped salad plates were used and went above the dinner plate – this meant that there could be no room for cutlery above the plate. We do not know why exactly the pudding fork and spoon migrated north, but you'll be safe in saying that the Americans are probably to blame. If conversation turns to salads or crockery in general, you could mention these now forgotten plates with a misty-eyed look and a slight sigh.

The position of the bread knife is divisive. Today it is more than likely to be found actually on the bread plate (the only knife to go on the left-hand side of the place setting). Traditionally, it would have been the outermost knife on the right-hand side and then moved to the bread plate. You might recall knowledgeably that this used to be the case.

Do say 'Do you remember those lovely salad plates you used to find?'

Don't say *(Picking up fork and spoon)* 'Shouldn't these go up there?'

GLASSES

Good dinner parties will see more than one type of wine served when at table. While many know that we use cutlery in a logical order (start from the outside and work in), an alarming many do not know the rule for glasses. It is very simple: work towards the back. Glasses are placed in order of use, and so the glass closest to the diner will be used first (perhaps the sherry glass to go with the soup). The water glass is placed slightly to the left, detached somewhat from the other glasses as it remains on the table throughout.

All wine will be served in decanters. Having bottles on the table will make it look like a takeaway.

PLATES AND SOUP PLATES

The keen eye will spot a total absence of 'chargers' from the refined British table. Although their presence is multiplying quickly, they are really not correct for British dining. If you do go out to dine somewhere you thought was a top-drawer kind of place and see such items, then leave immediately as it is not worth bothering to bluff. While even our most sophisticated cousins across the pond will use them, we in Britain do not need coasters for our plates.

The charger – sometimes called base plate or service plate – was introduced for American dining as they felt unable to come to a 'naked table' (a table with nothing in the centre of the setting…until the food arrived). The charger is set with the place setting, the first course is then placed on top with the charger framing the dinner plate. All very pretty but when questioned on the subject the bluffer should say that they just don't have the space to store these things and, even if they did, what's the point? (This will be taken as false modesty by your fellow diners who will assume that, like them, you have 14 bedrooms and 12 reception rooms.)

All plates should be round. Square plates are the reserve of gimmicky restaurants desperately trying to be voguish and have no place in a private home. Look at them with a faint air of bewilderment if your host places them at your setting. Also assume that when the soup course arrives it will be in a rimmed soup plate rather than a bowl – items that are not correct in formal dining. Only dogs eat out of bowls.

Napkin rings also have no place in formal dining. The Victorian middle classes introduced them to show whose napkin was whose as they would actually reuse their napkins for several consecutive meals (due to fewer staff and less money), and so patterns and designs varied to quasi-territorially mark out each person's linen. Now you can buy rings of uniform design for purely decorative purposes. There is no need to balk at seeing such items if you do stumble across them. Just remove your napkin from the ring, place it to the side of the setting, and remember to wash your hands at least twice when you are next in the lavatory.

Some tables – even the best tables – will have fish cutlery. This remains a bit of a grey area for would-be etiquette experts. Buckingham Palace does not use such things; however, many other well-known and aristocratic households do. Fifty years ago they were considered to be a bit common – as they, too, were an invention of the Victorian

middle classes (who had to have a piece of cutlery for everything). Now, many have come to like them for the aesthetics and so use them to spruce up their table.

HOLDING YOUR WEAPONS

The bluffer needs to consider how he holds his cutlery. The biggest error will be holding the knife like a pen. Not only does this not give the diner full control over what is on the

plate in front of them, but it will show them up as an impostor; they will only have themselves to blame when a bit of boeuf bourguignon goes scudding across the table quicker than they can say 'social suicide'.

Few people know the reason why you hold a wine glass by the stem and not the bowl, so this will give you maximum kudos should you be asked. The reason is simple. Holding the bowl transfers the heat from your hand to the glass and into the wine. Red wine is served *chambré* (room temperature) and white wine is served gently chilled. The heat from your hand will affect the temperature of the liquid inside and wine buffs (bluffers or otherwise) will be justifiably horrified. For further information on this vital area of dinner party etiquette, consult *The Bluffer's Guide to Wine*.

If staff are overseeing the service of your dinner, they may start serving in a totally different manner to that the bluffer is used to – especially if that bluffer has once worked in a restaurant. Food will be served and cleared from the left-hand side. Resist jumping suddenly when an arm extends from the left to clear your soup plate. The international standard (for reasons no one is that clear about) is to clear from the right; however, British private houses still set and clear from the left – for the logical reason that the glasses are on the right and you may knock them over. All drink is served from the right-hand side of the diner and whatever you do, don't hold out your glass to your left as your neighbour's is being replenished.

Don't say 'What ho, Jeeves! Didn't see you there.'

Do say (*To host/fellow diner*) 'So nice to see the old standard being maintained; so many restaurants or houses one goes to these days don't seem to have any standard whatsoever.'

KNOW YOUR CHINA

Should your hostess ask you to help clear, resist the urge to stack the plates. You will most likely be dining from fine Sèvres china or something similar and clumsily stacking the plates will scratch the delicate pattern – not something that you want to do or be seen to do. It shows that you are not used to dining from fine china.

DESSERT RATS

The final course of a dinner (and arguably the best one) is the pudding. Note, it is called the pudding. P-U-D-D-I-N-G. NOT 'dessert'! Many have started calling the sweet course that follows the main course the dessert as they think it sounds 'posher' (as it is an obviously French word rather than a clunky Anglo-Saxon-sounding one). In actual fact, pudding comes from another French word, *boudin*. In formal British dining, as represented by *Downton Abbey*, the dessert was a separate course that followed the pudding. Meals were much longer and stodgier back then and so a piece of fruit (an apple, pear, banana or orange) was served on a plate to act as a palate cleanser. At this stage the tablecloths were often 'drawn' or – at the very least – the wine glasses and any leftover cutlery and crockery were taken away if the cloths were to be left. This was 'dessert', as it was served after everything had been cleared from the table. If etymology is one of your interests, you will know that the word derives from the French *desservir*, as in the opposite of 'serve'. This sort of knowledge never fails to fascinate fellow diners.

Incidentally, if you call your lemon posset with spun sugar basket a dessert when dining with the hoity toity, then you might as well prepare for a future dining at a Toby Carvery – where you can help yourself to the dessert buffet for the rest of eternity.

ACT III: THE FINAL HOUR

We're in the second decade of the twenty-first century. Sexual equality has progressed to a degree unimaginable 100 years ago, when women in the UK didn't even have the vote. But when your meal ends, feminist bluffers had best make sure they're fully stoked on the diazepam as, open-mouthed, they watch the women repair into the drawing room to discuss tittle-tattle while the men stay behind to discuss politics. Do not create a scene by attempting to challenge this. You will not win. Gender equality has evolved as fully as it is ever going to as far as the British upper classes are concerned. Different rules apply in the dining and drawing rooms of great houses, and everybody from the loftiest and most formidable of dowagers to the lowliest of scullery maids knows their place.

While the women begin coffee service and perhaps some liqueurs, the men will drink port. The decanter will be placed by the butler in front of the guest of honour, who pours his own helping before passing to his left to the host, who does the same and also passes to his left. Whatever you do, don't pass it to the right and don't forget to pass it after you're finished pouring. The decanter circulates a couple more times during the 20 minutes or so the men and women are apart. If someone forgets to pass the decanter, there is a subtle way the bluffer can prompt resumed service:

Don't say 'Could you please pass the port?'

Do say 'Do you know the Bishop of Norwich?'

This is known by many as a gentle reminder (without saying exactly what the offence is) to the chap in question to buck his ideas up. If he replies 'No' to your question then you simply reply, 'He was a lovely chap but always forgot to pass the port'. This should then make it very clear to him.

Once they have returned home, slept and risen refreshed, the best guests will put pen to paper and write a thank-you letter on their engraved letter-headed writing paper. Black or blue ink are the options (the former being the more traditional), and the letter will show gratitude and graciousness towards your hosts and pretty much guarantee a return visit. An email just won't do.

'The world was my oyster but I used the wrong fork.'

Oscar Wilde

SPAGHETTIQUETTE (THE PROPER WAY TO EAT)

Food can be quite tricky to eat, and in some cases it's not just as simple as a knife and fork. A good bluffer in the world of etiquette must know how to eat these 'tricky foods' without making a fool of themselves.

Apples When served at table, usually as the dessert course, these are eaten with special cutlery for fruit: dessert cutlery. Cut the apple into quarters, scoop out the core and cut into chunks. The same applies for pears.

Artichokes Start by peeling off each artichoke leaf (fingers permitted) and dip into the sauce, then use your teeth to pull off the 'flesh' of the leaf. Discard leaves on the side of the plate. Then, when down to the tougher leaves and 'choke', use a knife and fork to gain access to the 'heart'.

Asparagus If served as a first course, rather than an accompaniment vegetable, these are eaten with the left hand and dipped into the hollandaise sauce. Making comments such as, 'This is jolly messy' or, 'Do we not get cutlery with this?' when eating such finger foods will expose you immediately as a bluffer.

Bananas Cut both ends off with dessert cutlery, slice down the skin to unwrap, and then cut off slices and eat with a fork and knife.

Bread Never cut a bread roll. Break a bite-sized chunk off, butter if desired, and eat. It is not the done thing to divide the bread into two, slather with butter and gnaw away. Don't be caught out as an air-butterer – apply the butter to the roll on the plate, not in the air.

Burgers Burgers, like sandwiches, were designed to be eaten using our hands. Yet restaurants are now serving burgers so large that they are impossible to pick up and eat elegantly. In this instance, they can be eaten with a knife and fork. Simply remove the top half of the bun and cut away, as per normal. The top bun can be cut into throughout the course. This is the exception to the no-bread-cutting rule above.

Canapés Nothing annoys sophisticates more than having to cope with canapés the size of door wedges. If your host offers you one of those gargantuan bruschetta things, you have two options: leave it, or try to tackle it as elegantly as possible. Remember that the other guests will have the same problem and so you will all look as foolish as each other. Correctly sized canapés can be popped into the mouth with ease and eaten in one go.

Cheese Never cut the 'nose' (point) off a triangular cheese; retain the original shape by cutting from the rind. A good bluffer will be able to explain why this is so; cheeses are made in the round before being divided up into triangles, and the cheesemakers consider the centre to be the best part. Cutting the nose off is taking the best bit just for yourself – which is very bad manners.

Grapes Resist picking off one grape at a time. Pull off a small branch with your hands, place on your plate and then pick off one by one. Grape scissors are sometimes at hand in Non-U houses to aid with this, and you might remark, 'How novel' when they are offered.

Kebabs The kebab skewer is a method of cooking, not of eating. Hold the kebab skewer in one hand and with your fork slide all of the chunks of meat one by one onto the plate and proceed to eat normally.

Mussels The most elegant method is to use a fork to loosen and consume the first mollusc within, before using the empty shell to tweeze out the other mussels, discarding redundant shells on a nearby plate.

Oysters A skilled high-society *habitué* will know that these are only eaten in months containing the letter R. The upmarket way to eat is to simply tip the contents into the mouth from the shell, having loosened the contents beforehand with a fork. An oyster fork is a Victorian middle-class invention and does nothing a normal fork cannot do. If an oyster fork is set, use it. If not, just use a normal small fork. Never ask for an oyster fork or that will set you into a class of your own. Goat class!

Pasta Try to avoid cutting pasta if at all possible.

Peas Your host will never serve these at a formal dinner party, but if you find yourself confronted by *petit pois* then resist the urge to put your fork into the right hand, turn it over and scoop. Instead, use the tines of the fork to spear a collection and transfer to the mouth. If mashed potato has been served, or something similar, use that as a 'glue'. Complaining about this tiresome technique of eating (rather than the scoop method) is not the done thing.

Pizza Italians will eat this with their hands in informal dining, and so this is perfectly acceptable. If it's a sloppy pizza then stick to cutlery and just cut small chunks off at a time.

Salad Best practice with salad says not to cut it. Nobody quite knows how this practice came about, or why it is 'best'. It might have something to do with primitive, old metal knife blades discolouring leaves. There are no hard and fast rules about salad cutting. If the salad is too large to eat without cutting then you may cut it with impunity, with either knife or fork, or both.

Salt and pepper Salt should never be scattered all over your food. Instead, place in a pile on the side of the plate and dip food into it. Pepper, on the other hand, may be scattered hither and yon. If salt comes in a mill, however, then it may go everywhere. Do not ask for salt and pepper if it is not on the table. There might be a reason for this, such as the cook holding strong views on the matter.

Soup Soup is always 'eaten', never drunk. The soup spoon is held in the right hand and scoops away from you on one side, skimming the surface. Then sip from the nearside of the spoon. Tipping the bowl away from you at the end to help you catch the last few mouthfuls is perfectly fine. A good conversational piece, if the right moment arises, is to comment on how you are so glad soup is now eaten with smaller, oval soup spoons (NB: not so long ago, soup was consumed in the same fashion as today, but using tablespoons).

Spaghetti This is eaten with a fork alone and never cut with a knife. The idea of using a spoon as well comes from the USA but is not practised in authentic Italian homes or upmarket British ones. Spaghetti can be messy, so avoid ordering this on a date or when dining with clients.

Steak Resist smothering your steak in any sauce that might accompany it; instead, decant the sauce from the pot onto the side of the plate with a knife and cut one chunk of steak at a time and dip into sauce. A steak knife will come in handy here.

Tomato sauce With anything like this, place a small bit on the side of the plate, rather than sloshing it all over your food. Sauces should be served in glass bowls or ramekins, but never served during formal dining. Again, if it is not on the table, don't ask for it.

Toast Many people now have adopted the rather heathen fashion of spreading slices of toast with butter and then jam or marmalade. But toast, just like other breads, should not be smothered or cut. Instead, break a small chunk off, garnish, and then eat. If you eat your toast incorrectly when you are a house guest in a U household, you will not be invited back.

DON'T WEAR
BROWN IN TOWN

As has already been noted, people are judged within the first few seconds of meeting. What one wears plays a big part in said judgement; keen eyes will be taking in what you are wearing to ascertain whether you are polished or *parvenu*.

WHITE TIE

The most formal of evening dress codes, and correctly called 'full evening dress', white tie is a dying breed. To impress when discussing the subject, you should advocate its return as 'it does look very smart', although 'a bit of a faff to get into' (this last bit is especially needed if the bluffer is male). Many will know of white tie from the dining scenes of *Downton Abbey*, or press pictures from the biannual state dinners at Buckingham Palace or Windsor Castle. You should make sure that it is subtly known that you have experienced it personally rather than from your sofa on a Sunday evening.

FOR HIM

Top hat Even though white tie is the dressiest of the dress codes, in modern times the top hat is a bit much, really. If you do insist on sporting one, then it should be silk and collapsible – a nod to the days when gentlemen would have to store them under their seats at the opera. Also remember that a gentleman never wears his hat indoors.

Bow tie The clue is in the title of the dress code: a white bow tie (hand-tied) is correct. Make sure your hands are spotless before tying, as the brilliant white of the tie will show every grubby mark unforgivingly. Waiters serving at a white tie event will wear a black bow tie in order to mark themselves out from the guests. The bluffer does not want to look like a waiter. Heaven forbid!

Shirt A white, winged collar (detachable from the dress shirt) should adorn the top of the dress shirt, which should be fastened with dress studs: white mother of pearl does the job nicely. Cuffs should be double-cuffed (i.e., with cufflinks). The shirt should be starched to within an inch of its life.

Jacket The black (sometimes midnight blue) tailcoat is double-breasted, although never fastened, and should just show a hint of the white waistcoat beneath. A gentleman should not sit on the tails but carefully part them when taking one's seat; a theatrical flick of the tails is the reserve of concert pianists and should be avoided.

Waistcoat This is low-cut, double-breasted and in piqué honeycomb with a shawl collar. All buttons are fastened.

Trousers Black and tapered with two pieces of braid running down the side of each leg, they should be held in place with the aid of braces, never a belt.

Socks Long, black, silk evening socks are preferable, although merino wool is an acceptable modern alternative (but not quite the same).

Shoes Patent black and without toe caps. Always lace-ups.

FOR HER

Women have rules to follow, too, although not as many as men. Whereas their male counterparts find it a bit of a faff with the finery of full evening dress (especially if they should be unfortunate enough not to have a valet), women generally throw themselves wholeheartedly into the process.

Hair Long, flowing hair is not correct; it should be worn 'up' and well restrained to avoid lashing dancing partners during the tango.

Tiaras If the occasion calls for such

items then they may be worn…but only by married women. Never buy a tiara. If you haven't had one handed down through the generations (chances are you won't have), resist the urge to make the purchase. You'll be buying your own furniture next.

Dresses Sadly, 'dresses to the floor' has a different, rather

'Never dress down for the poor.
They won't respect you for it.'

Imelda Marcos

louche meaning in twenty-first-century Britain, but for white tie, dresses should be sweeping and 'to the floor' (i.e., floor length). Younger women with slightly more supple skin opt for sleeveless gowns, whereas older women prefer longer sleeves to hide less, er, toned arms.

Gloves Long gloves should be worn at all times, except when dining when they are removed and placed in the lap, with napkin on top.

Jewellery Rings are worn under the gloves, bracelets go on top. Earrings are long in the evening.

Shoes Closed-toe shoes are correct and are worn over tights.

MORNING DRESS

Morning dress is a daytime dress code and generally worn for Royal Ascot, smart weddings and funerals, garden parties and the like. Call it a 'morning suit' at your peril.

FOR HIM

Top hat Black or grey top hats are optional at weddings but compulsory in the Royal Enclosure at Ascot.

Shirt A turndown collar is correct here. White is generally the preferred colour. A pale pastel colour may be toyed with by fashionistas.

Tie Always a tie. Foulards and cravats are mainly seen at downmarket weddings.

Coat (jacket) A curve-fronted, tailed, single-breasted number, usually in black or grey. If attending Ladies' Day at Ascot, then grey is *de rigueur*.

Waistcoat Bright colours are to be treated with care and perhaps best reserved for younger wedding guests. Grey or buff/camel waistcoats are the better options. Black could be worn for very formal or sombre occasions.

Gloves A bit of a nuisance, but needed. The grey, white or lemon gloves are correctly carried, not worn.

Trousers The most important thing to remember here

is that they do not match the material or design of the coat. They are held up by braces and are usually a lighter, pinstriped grey. Darker ones can look like they've been hired in.

Shoes Formal, well-polished (but not patent), black lace-ups. Brogues or loafers just won't do.

Accessories A *boutonnière* in the lapel is permissible for the florally inclined, and a pocket square may also be sported, but probably not at the same time – that may be overkill.

FOR HER

Hats Straw hats are permissible after Easter. Fascinators remain a sartorial hot potato. Female bluffers should steer well clear of them. Even though the younger generations are slightly fonder of them, you won't go far wrong with a proper hat. No hat at all and, as Prime Minister David Cameron's wife Samantha once found to her peril, you will fall prey to wagging tongues. Make sure you remove your hat at 6pm – especially important if at a wedding breakfast where the festivities continue into the evening.

Dresses For formal daywear, dresses can be colourful and, depending on the season, will be of varying materials. White and black should be avoided for weddings: the former will clash with the bride and the latter, unless heavily broken up, is too funereal. Nothing above the knee, really.

Gloves A must!

Tights Ladder-free, or else you run the risk of looking like a lady of the night.

Shoes These may have a heel, but anything over a couple of inches is a tad tarty and not practical for standing for long periods.

BLACK TIE

This is a dress code for evening events and social functions after 6pm. It is less formal than white tie but more formal than informal or business dress.

FOR HIM

Shirt A white dress shirt with a turned-down collar is called for with black tie. Winged collars, often mistakenly worn, are now the reserve of the white-tie dress code. Dress shirts can be fastened with buttons or studs. Cuffs should be double-cuffed (i.e., with cufflinks).

Bow tie Black tie does not mean a black necktie; they are for funerals and actors at awards ceremonies. Bow ties should be hand-tied (Her Majesty The Queen is said to be able to spot a 'fake', pre-tied bow tie a mile off). If you cannot tie one, then it is suggested you learn, or try to look good in a pre-tied one (impossible).

FAQ *Can I remove my dinner jacket at an event?*

A gentleman never removes his jacket. You may take it off once home or in your guest suite and after the curtains have been drawn.

Jacket Black or sometimes blue-black jackets can be single- or double-breasted with either peaked or shawl lapels. Dinner jackets are never fastened when single-breasted. Unlike daytime suit jackets, dinner jackets have no vents at the back and the buttons are 'covered'.

FAQ *Is it all right to wear a white dinner jacket?*

White dinner jackets are permissible in very tropical climes and should only be worn with a shawl collar. If you wear a white jacket outside of tropical climes then people may look at you with suspicion or – worse – confuse you with the barman. Surrey is not a tropical clime.

Pocket square If you do wear a 'top-pocket handkerchief' (sometimes called a pochette), then you may wear a white one. It should be worn in a plume, without the corners of the handkerchief showing. Anything other than this will mark you out as a phony.

Cummerbund Worn around the waist instead of a waistcoat, cummerbunds seem sadly consigned to formalwear obscurity. The folds should point upwards.

Braces Don't wear a belt, even if hidden by a cummerbund. Instead, opt for braces, preferably black, if you need to keep your trousers up.

Trousers These should match the material of the jacket and are usually tapered slightly, with one braid running down the outside of each leg.

Socks Black silk evening socks are technically correct but are not widely sold, and most people are opting to wear conventional black wool or cotton socks. Every effort should be made to try to source the silk variety.

'There is one other reason for dressing
well, namely that dogs respect it,
and will not attack you in good clothes.'
Ralph Waldo Emerson

Shoes Well-polished, smart black shoes are perfectly acceptable. If you have black patent leather shoes, then wear them instead.

Accessories Visible timepieces are technically not worn (although a discreet wristwatch is now acceptable) because black-tie events are not something in which timekeeping is a priority. White gloves and scarves are a bit OTT nowadays and were only worn when travelling to and from the venue. If you opt to wear them at the actual event, then you should be prepared to be the subject of quizzical looks all evening.

FAQ *Can I wear a red bow tie?*

No.

FOR HER

Hair If there is to be dancing, then it is worn 'up' if long.

Dresses Any dress that stops somewhere between floor length or just below the knee is fine. Wear as much or as little colour as you want; the object of the men wearing just black and white is so that the women will stand out and look radiant. If there is more 'back' on display then there should be less 'front', and vice versa.

Shoes Closed-toe.

LOUNGE SUITS (AKA BUSINESS ATTIRE)

FOR HIM

Colour Suits should be in grey or navy. A black suit is not the done thing and bluffers should avoid them at all costs. A brown suit is simply beyond the pale for citywear.

Stripes, checks or plain? The choice of pattern is up to the wearer. Stripes complement the taller man's stature but should be treated with caution by the shorter man – and never worn outside major cities. In all cases stripes should be 'pin' not 'chalk', and checks should be 'quiet' not 'loud'.

Jacket Two- or three-button suits are correct. One button should only ever be fastened. On a two-button suit the top one is fastened when standing; on a three-button the middle button is fastened only. All buttons are unfastened when seated to avoid strain. Fastening your jacket incorrectly is a clear sign to everyone that you are a *parvenu* and not to be trusted.

Jacket sleeve buttons Maximum bluffing points will be awarded if your buttons on the sleeves are real ('working'). You can show off your working suit sleeves when washing your hands in public lavatories: unbutton and roll back both jacket and shirt sleeve and then fasten again.

Shirt This should be a turndown collar; button-down collars (practically a craze in the USA) are not correct British formalwear and should not be worn with a tie.

Shirtsleeves Double-cuff or button cuffs are fine – the former being dressier and slightly more formal. If double-cuffs are worn then you require cufflinks. Novelty cufflinks are not to be encouraged under any circumstances.

Tie design This is where a bluffer can come unstuck. Striped ties often have associations with military regiments or public schools. Unless you are an alumnus of either then avoid wearing their tie or else you will be seen as an impostor – which is the unacceptable side of bluffing. You can't go wrong with a plain tie.

Tie style Skinny ties are to be avoided and look as if one can't afford a proper one. Stick to a wider tie (otherwise referred to as 'normal') to keep from looking offbeat.

Tie length The tie should finish just above the waistband of the trousers.

Braces Savile Row regulars will know that braces, rather than clunky belts, make smart trousers hang much better and so you should always wear them. No one will ever see the colour of the braces as a man does not remove his jacket in polite company.

Belt If braces are to be shunned and black shoes are worn, then the belt should be black (leather). And, you've guessed it: brown shoes – brown belt.

Socks Ideally they should be knee-length socks. They are becoming much harder to find but shops on Jermyn Street in London are the answer.

Shoes A lady will say she can tell a lot about a man from his shoes and so they should be well-kept at all times; polish them regularly and replace the laces when the aglets (the plastic bit on the end of laces) fall off or begin to fray. Wearing brown shoes with a business suit is Italian practice but not the done thing in British society. Brown shoes are to be reserved for the country.

FOR HER

Jewellery If jewellery is to be worn it should be subtle and restricted to one or two items. Wrists laden with bangles and bracelets that clatter every time you move your hand will be distracting and irritating to colleagues.

Cleavage Less is more.

Blouses and shirts Make sure they are not too tight and are in pristine condition.

Skirts Not too short, please! Anything above the knee is too short.

Hosiery A real lady never goes without tights or stockings. Ensure that they are ladder-free.

Shoes Very high heels or open-toed shoes are not office-appropriate, but heels may be fine for certain evening social functions.

SMART CASUAL

The smarter set's casual get-up is not as well groomed as many think (although the younger generations are beginning to change this). A good bluffer will emulate the general principle of looking well polished and slick when dressed formally (full evening dress through to a suit) but not as together when relaxing. Jeans are not really worn by the upper classes unless under the age of 40. Denim post-40 shouts 'middle class, midlife, midriff crisis' of the type regularly exemplified by portly TV presenters such as Jeremy Clarkson. Another 'look' to steer well clear of is the round-neck-t-shirt-under-shirt look. Simply dreadful.

Again, and this is a key point that may be too much for some, do remember not to wear brown shoes in London – unless, of course, it is a Friday or weekend, when you will be either going to the country post-work, or have come into town from the country for the weekend. In the best social circles this rule is still observed. Even with jeans or chinos on a Tuesday, wear black shoes…or any colour other than brown. Just remember: don't wear brown in town.

A WORD ON TATTOOS AND PIERCINGS

Wife of the prime minister and daughter of a baronet, Samantha Cameron has a tattoo in the shape of a dolphin, which she unwisely elected to have applied to her ankle while an undergraduate at Bristol Polytechnic (before it became the University of the West of England). She probably regrets it now. 'SamCam' is a slight exception when it comes to tattoos and the upper classes. They normally abhor and shun them. You should do the same. If you already have tattoos, either cover them up or save up for the surgery to get them removed. Your attitude regarding these things should be that while you respect people's right to be disfigured by so-called 'body art', it is also your right to point out that an arm that resembles a public lavatory wall is not a good look.

As for piercings, anywhere other than through the earlobes is out of the question. Pierced navels, noses and nipples and, God forbid, anywhere near genitalia are signs of social degeneracy to the upper classes, who have only recently come to accept having their ears pierced. Before their epiphany the attitude was very much 'if God had wanted us to have holes in our ears he would have put them there'.

'Twitter makes you like people you've never met. Facebook makes you hate those you've known all your life.'

Anon

TWITTIQUETTE

The old guard has come late to the online world and social networking sites, yet there is still a significant percentage who use it. Conducting yourself online in the correct and proper manner has never been more important, with future bosses, partners and friends very likely to check out your social and professional credentials before any invitations to join The Firm or attend a dinner party are offered.

Don't say 'I am such a Facebook stalker!'

Do say 'Do I do social networking? Of course – I attended the hunt ball last weekend.'

EMAIL

While the aristocracy like nothing more than putting pen to paper, email is now very much part of their lives and has been universally adopted. Even the Queen is reported to use email. Don't expect the uppers to be firing off an e-missive on their state-of-the-art tablets, while wearing a Bluetooth headset as they partake in a chukka of polo. Oh no, their emailing will be done on a rickety old machine that makes an abacus look cutting edge.

Do say 'An iPad? An old mobile phone is as far as I go, I'm afraid.'

Don't say 'Can't wait to get an iPad but I'm waiting for Apple to release the updated hardware so I can fully enjoy the retina display.'

Spending money on gadgets and gizmos (and do feel free to call them that) is a bizarre, alien concept to the upper classes. You should adopt the same attitude: you'd rather spend the money on something useful, like a new horse, than on something called a Google Glass. Your second-hand PC from 2003, with the M key missing, is fine and will see you out for a few more years yet.

Correct etiquette with emails is the same as with a conventional letter. If you start with 'Dear Sir', you should end with 'Yours faithfully'. Where you put the name of a person (e.g., 'Dear Mr Hamilton'), then you end with 'Yours sincerely'. If you start with 'Hi there', you can end in any way you want. But don't necessarily expect a reply.

As for an email address, it should be something conservative and understated. If your email handle happens to be something remotely interesting, then change it immediately. Only your name will do. You cannot go about emailing Lady Bracknell with an email such as 'princess_gaby_x@hotmail.com'. Unless, of course, you are in fact a real princess. But then, if you were, your name wouldn't be Gaby.

HUGS AND KISSES

Ending an email or text with a queue of hugs (O) and kisses (X) is wholly unnecessary. Remember that the British – especially those of better breeding – do not enjoy showing emotion either in person or digitally. One kiss is sufficient; two kisses may be permissible for closer friends. But remember: never put a kiss on the end of an email or text to someone if you wouldn't actually kiss them in real life.

TWITTER

For the old guard, Twitter is really the reserve of a younger generation, or over 40s whose political compass points left. If you're not already in or on Twitter, don't bother joining. If you are, just watch what you tweet. The slightest spelling mistake or grammatical error and your waiting followers will pounce on it and savage you – a trend popularised by the former red-top editor Piers Morgan.

Now you might begin to understand that Twitter is no respecter of etiquette. As with all social media, attention-seeking posts are to be avoided at all costs as they will show you up to be a lightweight. They also can convey far too much emotion and, as discussed elsewhere in this guide, this is something to be discouraged. We are frightfully pleased you have a new job, or new car, or that you've given birth, but all such life achievements should be underplayed and written about in a casual, offhand manner in order to show that you are above such things as melodrama.

FACEBOOK

The undisputed king of the social network world but also the Duke of Windsor of the online community, in the sense that it may not reign for long.

Watch your friend count – too many and you look needy and shallow. It is not a competition, and all the best people avoid Facebook, anyway. Advanced etiquette bluffers clearly don't do (or have time for) social networking.

Online games via Facebook such as FarmVille are for people with more time than sense on their hands (not to mention they are now *so* three years ago).

If you do use Facebook, any major design changes must be met by you with major irritation. You do not like change in life, especially when it comes to web-page design, as you had only just worked out how to navigate the last 'site map' and don't have time to learn the new way.

Never make the mistake of using Facebook language in polite company. Anybody who does so should be immediately deleted from your 'friend' list. This is known as 'defriending', arguably one of the most unpleasant recent additions to the English language... apart from 'poke', which is even more intolerable.

LINKEDIN

Business-based networking sites such as LinkedIn pose an interesting conundrum for scions of the great families of Olde England. They have always had a job/role in the family business or on the family estate, so why on earth would they want to be on a social media upstart like

LinkedIn? Or, for the very rich, why would they need any job at all? Yet the younger members of the top strata of society now actively seek jobs and many need them, as the family fortune might not be what it once was.

Note that your picture on the profile page should never be a cropped headshot of one of your holiday snaps. It simply isn't appropriate, however golden and lithe you look. No picture at all would be the better option, but the ideal is something professional-looking and in business attire.

DROPBOX

File-sharing sites like Dropbox are totally unheard of and never used by the upper sets, who prefer just to print files out to store (they don't really 'do' rainforests).

Don't say 'Yes, I can't get enough of Dropbox!'

Do say 'Dropbox? Certainly not. What are the symptoms?'

PICTURE POSTS

Posting pictures via Instagram, Twitter or even just on Facebook is a good way to assert your new social status, but it still must be handled with tact and discretion. Display too many images of Bollinger Champagne set against a poolside in Monaco and you will be seen as a social bore and a bit naff. Why take and post pictures of something that all your other friends are doing anyway?'

You can be clever, however, with your pictures. You could broadcast a picture of something unassuming, like you serving breakfast, but the plates in the shot are nothing but the finest Limoges. Or you could Instagram a picture of your jacket wardrobe – naturally they will all be from Savile Row or Jermyn Street and only fellow aficionados of better breeding will be able to tell. Or rather than taking a picture of the splendid grandfather clock in the lower guard chamber (what lesser houses call 'the hall') and adding the caption 'grandfather clock', wait until 6pm, take a picture of it then and post with the caption 'Amontillado o'clock!' That way, you are not only showing off your lovely clock but also just reaffirming to everyone that you're a connoisseur of fine sherry, rather than something lower middle class like an alcopop.

Flowers or plants from the garden (which you should call 'the grounds' or 'the gardens') are always good pictures to post, too. Especially if you caption them using the Latin name.

ETIQUETTE
WHEN HATCHED

Giving birth is reportedly one of the most painful experiences a woman can endure. Yet if the birth announcement is worded incorrectly in the paper the following week, the pain of being shunned by your aristocratic associates will be almost as bad.

The first thing to know is that in the upper classes you have a child (or several) to carry on 'the line'. It is of course your duty to procreate, but it is no longer the done thing to worry about carrying on the family 'name', possibly because these days it can't be guaranteed. You might have heard about 'primogeniture', an ancient feudal rule in England ensuring that the eldest son inherited the family estate (and any title if relevant), and that if there was no immediate male successor then the daughters would pick up the pieces. It's all terribly *Downton* and terribly old hat, except in the case of the British monarchy, where it still prevails – although we're assured that it's all going to change, and that soon your gender will make no difference to where you rank in line to the throne – an astonishingly progressive thought!

Do say 'Thank goodness they're finally sorting this out.'

Don't say 'Do I still get the loot? What is primogeniture anyway?'

Maximum bluffing value Primogeniture was intended to preserve larger estates from being broken up, and thus weakening the power of the nobility. It prevailed throughout England until the mid-twentieth century, although it was never observed in the county of Kent and it never made it over the pond to the USA.

(You might also bear in mind that women are still ineligible to succeed to the majority of hereditary peerages in Britain. But nobody ever claimed that the aristocracy moved quickly in these matters.)

Mothers-to-be must treat their pregnancy as a duty, too. Complaining too much about the baby kicking, tossing and turning in the womb is a tad downmarket. Acting as if you are the first woman in the world to be pregnant will only cause eyes to roll.

Don't say 'Oh, it's kicking off again! God, I'd like a glass of fizz.'

Do say (*with a sigh*) 'It's all just a bit boring, really.'

Expectant mothers should carry on with normal activities as long as possible. You want to be the 'How does she do it?' woman. Dress impeccably, smile and be your usual charming self, and when it does all begin to get too much, don't leave the house and accept no callers except immediate family. The pregnant bluffer should ensure that pregnancy becomes them and that they should never be seen to be anything other than radiant and glowing.

BIRTH ANNOUNCEMENTS

Placing an announcement in a national newspaper (*The Times* and/or *The Daily Telegraph*) is the traditional route and is the duty of the father, together with telephoning close relatives. In modern times a Facebook post or a tweet, or even a round-robin text to announce the birth, is also just about acceptable – especially with fewer people reading newspapers nowadays and the extortionate rates editors charge for such notices. Yet better families will ensure that regardless of what modern methods of communications are at their disposal, the traditional way will also be observed, as 'it's so much nicer for the child to look back on when they grow up, don't you think?'

The correct form for printed announcements is:

SMYTHE – On 9th September, to Richard and Elizabeth, a daughter.

Mentioning the hospital name, ward, name of the child, and sentiments like 'much-needed sister for Rollo, Nico, Hugo and Theo' are not correct, although frequently seen.

The form for announcements of the birth of a child to a single mother is:

SMITH – On 10th September, to Debbie, a son.

NAMING YOUR CHILD

If you want your child to be accepted into the higher social circles you have bluffed your way into, then think carefully about what you name him or her. You may desperately want to choose something offbeat and quirky like 'Tad' (short for 'Tadpole'), but the best people have two catalogues of names from which to pick: Biblical or Royal – which often prove to be the same thing.

'To create is divine,
to reproduce is human.'

Man Ray

Although there are many more options available, you won't go wrong with any of the following:

Adam, Alexandra, Andrew, Angela, Anna, Anne, Benjamin, Camilla, Charles, Claudia, Daniel, David, Deborah, Diana, Edward, Elizabeth, Harold, Henry, James, John, Jonathan, Lily, Mark, Mary, Matthew, Michael, Paul, Paula, Peter, Philip, Phoebe, Richard, Sarah, Simeon, Simon, Stephen, Susanna(h), Thomas, Timothy, Victoria, William.

It's always a good idea to check the Office for National Statistics for the current year's rankings of most popular baby names before branding the benighted child for life. Avoid anything in the top 10, and arguably in the top 100. Name him Harry or George or her Amelia or Grace in the next couple of years, and the chances are that he/she will be among six or seven similarly named in the same classroom, office, dinner party, whatever for the rest of their lives. For the same reason avoid calling him Hugo, Sonny, Seth, Elliott, Theodore, Rory or Ellis; or her Mollie, Ivy, Darcey, Tilly, Florence or Violet, all in the top 100 in 2013, knocking out Joel, Hayden, John, Ashton, Jackson, Ben and Reece, and Lexie, Lauren, Rebecca, Tia, Nicole and Kayla.

There are some interesting names in the Bible such as Aaron, Bethany and Ethan. But even these have now passed from U to Non-U. Apologies to any aspiring social climbers with those names, but your parents clearly weren't thinking properly, and the going rate for a deed poll is only £33.

You may be in the position of being told of a future or just-born baby's bizarre name by someone who until that moment you thought was fairly sound on this sort of thing. Good manners dictate that you should not scoff or make a pithy comment, however much you want to.

Don't say 'Miele? As in the vacuum cleaner?'

Do say 'Miele, you say? What a lovely name!'

BREASTFEEDING

Still a hot potato, breastfeeding is ideally done in private. While a mother arguably has every right to expose a breast in public to feed her child, the whole process can make observers uncomfortable, and good manners generally state that anything that does unnerve or upset people should be avoided.

At parties, the more thoughtful host will offer a private room to the lactating mother should she wish to feed the child.

Art critic and broadcaster Brian Sewell, in a debate with a pro-public breastfeeding campaigner, unwittingly illustrated the depth of ignorance on the subject when he was reported to have said: 'Madam! How would you like it if I got my d**k out in the National Gallery?' No doubt he was unaware that breasts aren't genitals.

CHRISTENING PARTIES V BABY SHOWERS

If invited to a baby shower, you should ask what one is. Always show a total lack of knowledge of such things, as within high society they are perceived to be a modern contrivance and thus hardly *comme il faut*. By all means attend one, but adopt a bewildered expression throughout most of the event and other like-minded people will be able to identify your feelings and will gravitate towards you.

Don't say 'I just love baby showers!'

Do say 'What's wrong with a normal bath, and why would it be a cause for celebration anyway?'

Brace yourself for 'fun' games such as 'Suss the Size of Mummy's Tummy' and 'Decorate a Onesie'.

There are two levels of baby showers: terrible and ghastly. The terrible ones will take place in someone's house. The ghastly ones take place at a hired venue where you will unfortunately find yourself in something called a 'function room'.

The Americans have given us these baby showers, where the expectant mother is 'showered' with gifts designed to help furnish the nursery. The British equivalent is a christening party, which happens post-birth after the christening (or, for the non-religious, 'naming ceremony').

Christening parties are much less cringe-inducing affairs. Unlike baby showers, where invitations may only extend to women, these parties will probably be for close family and friends, and usually the priest who officiated the service.

Gifts will be given at the christening party but probably just by grandparents, godparents and very close family. The idea is something 'that lasts'. The complete range of *Mr Men* and *Little Miss* books are not appropriate here. Instead, opt for something of some value – such as a silver photo frame, christening mug, perhaps a bottle of the year's port to be opened when the child comes of age or, if you really want to be original, maybe a work of art by an unknown young artist. You never know.

'It's been an emotional day. Even the cake is in tiers.'

Anon

ETIQUETTE
WHEN MATCHED

Weddings are incredibly stressful for most of the leading players, but for those who have got as far as marrying 'up', you will need to pay extra attention in order not to stumble upon woeful wedding class pitfalls that will make your special day look like something from the pages of *Hello!* magazine. Or even worse, *OK!* magazine.

The first challenge is obviously to ensure that you pick someone eminently suitable to marry – preferably someone who was eminent before your union was imminent. Hopefully, if this guide's advice has been followed to the letter, you will have been moving in the right circles and so this will not prove too difficult.

Your engagement should last somewhere between six months and a year. Anything shorter and you will forget to plan crucial details. You will also need sufficient time to ensure that there are no unpleasant surprises, such as (if you're the groom) the bride turning up at the church in a horse-drawn Cinderella carriage.

NEWSPAPER ENGAGEMENT NOTICES

It is essential that news of your engagement be published in a newspaper. Even if your betrothed argues that it is a waste of money, you must hold firm on sticking to tradition, as it will impress your future parents-in-law. Usual rules – *The Times* or *The Daily Telegraph*.

The wording is such:

> *Dr J.M.G. Hunter and Miss S.M. Smythe*
> *The engagement is announced between James, first son of Captain and Mrs R.V. Hunter, Tarporley, Cheshire, and Susan, only daughter of Mr and Mrs J.R.C. Smythe of Malpas, Cheshire.*

Technically, the bride's parents should pay for this and hopefully your insistence on old values will ensure that they do (though if you are the bride you may want to stay silent on this point).

STAG AND HEN PARTY DON'TS

When asked by friends whether you are having one of these, you should adopt a withering tone and reply, 'I don't think so, do you?' You can then say you each may host an intimate cocktail hour for respective friends a few days before the wedding, or even a quiet dinner out. But ill-advised trips to Prague (with or without gaffer tape and lamp posts) are not to be tolerated or even considered by anyone in their right mind.

Rescind the invitation of anyone who even suggests anything to do with pink fluffy bunny ears, cowgirl hats or balloons in the shape of phalluses. You do not want them at your wedding. They are more than likely to pass wind during the vows and fall about laughing.

WHEN TO MARRY

The smarter set prefers weddings at the height of the social season (April to end of July), although autumn weddings are not unheard of. And there is a lot to be said for the winter months, with holly and candles. But goosebumps don't look great in the wedding photos.

There is considerable bluffing potential in knowing that many Roman Catholic churches don't allow weddings during Lent (the season of penitence). The Church of England does, but no flowers may be present in the church. Best to wait until after Lent to marry for a full floral display, preferably under the auspices of florists by royal appointment, Moyses Stevens.

Smart church weddings begin at two o'clock or half past two. Any other time isn't really done. Registry office weddings can be earlier or later, but they tend not to be society affairs and thus normal rules of etiquette don't apply.

THE GUEST LIST

Think carefully about who you invite as they will be mixing with your soon-to-be spouse's friends and family, and you don't really want Uncle Gary turning up under the influence and letting the side down, do you? 'Gaz' is best left uninvited – or 'reception only' to limit his presence.

The bride and groom are each given 50% of the guest

list. The groom submits the names of his chosen family and friends to the parents of the bride, who are in charge of drawing up the guest list. It is better to have four reliable friends who won't try to steal the teaspoons rather than 100 in order to look popular.

THE INVITATIONS

Invitations (never 'invites') for weddings frequently have more money spent on them than the wedding dress. If you are to succeed in social bluffing, you must know that convention dictates that an invitation should be eight inches tall by six inches wide with engraved text.

Don't allow yourself to suggest that a wedding dress code could be anything other than morning dress.

The printing of the text is where people often come unstuck. Remember this simple rule: avoid thermography! It's seen as the cheaper version of engraving and never looks as good. The U guests will be running their fingers over the invitations the moment they arrive in the post to see what method of printing was chosen. (Note that flat printing is simply beyond the pale.)

Wedding invitations are portrait in style and look like greeting cards, although they only have printing on the outwards-facing side (the place where the 'design' would go on a greeting card) and nothing on the other three sides. Comments that this is a 'waste of paper' will not go down well with the wedding *cognoscenti*.

The dress code is not stated, as all church weddings are morning dress. Don't allow yourself to suggest that a wedding could be anything else. Some *arrivistes* have started marrying in black tie, an evening dress code, during the day. If anyone asks if the dress code is black tie, it is the done thing to assume they are joking and laugh heartily. Even if they were not, they should soon realise the error of their ways.

The standard wording is:

Mr and Mrs John Smythe
request the pleasure of your company
at the marriage of their daughter
Susan Mary
to
Dr James Michael Gregory Hunter
at St Peter's, Hale
on Saturday 17th May 2013
at two o'clock
and afterwards at
The Gables, Malpas

RSVP
The Gables
Malpas
Cheshire

Invitations should be sent out six to eight weeks in advance. As with normal formal invitations, guests reply within a few days of receiving, and by post or by hand, in the third person (Mr Richard Smith thanks Mr and Mrs John Smythe… etc.).

WEDDING RINGS

Men of the gentry and aristocracy do not wear rings (or, to be correct, wedding bands). Women, of course, do, and the ring goes on the fourth finger of the left hand.

Female bluffers must never refer to rings as 'rocks'. Or on the rocks is where their marriage to a gentrified groom is likely to end up.

BRIDAL SHOWERS

The general idea is that the bride is showered with must-have gifts to help her set up her home with her new husband. Just as with baby showers, your stance on these should be one of complete bewilderment as to what they are, what their purpose is and why anyone in their right mind would want one. They are the height of self-indulgence and if they are to be held, the bride or any of the bride's family should not be the hosts as it is seen as presumptuous.

GIFT REGISTRIES

A gift registry is different from a wedding 'wish' list in so far as it is limited to the stock of a specified retailer. Think very carefully about where you choose to have it because it can speak volumes about your taste. Avoid Debenhams and BHS. Opt instead for Selfridges, Harrods or The General Trading Company. John Lewis is the safe choice for those who don't want to appear too grasping.

Charity gift registries (where guests are asked to donate to charity) can be seen as a bit over-worthy. They might be acceptable for the Duke and Duchess of Cambridge, who are unlikely to be in need of anything to set up home, but few of us are likely to enjoy that degree of privilege and status.

Remember:

- The list must have items across a wide price range (not every member of the cut-glass-finger-bowl brigade has bottomless pockets).

- Do not print information about where the list is being held on the invitation.

- Guests are free to go 'off list'. Couples should welcome any gift with the same level of gratitude (and you can always recycle unwanted gifts to less important friends at a later date; everybody does it).

Requesting money instead of gifts is becoming more popular but avoid including naff messages (on or off the invitations) such as:

Because at first we lived in sin
We already have the kitchen bin
A gift from you would be swell
But we'd prefer a gift to our wishing well.

Believe it or not, there are preprinted invitations bearing such ghastly sentiments. Worse, they even have gaps for names, dates and venues to be inserted. These must be avoided at all costs. In fact, if you should receive an invitation of this sort, make your excuses and decline.

DRESS

For first-time brides, white is obviously the colour. Jokes about the irony of the bride wearing white when she is known to have been 'popular' pre-engagement are best avoided. Second-time brides will often introduce other colours (nothing too adventurous) or marry in a smart suit in a much more low-key affair.

The groom's party must wear morning dress. (For a detailed description of this smart formal daytime dress code, *see* page 41.)

RECEIVING LINE AT RECEPTION

All the best weddings have a receiving line for guests at the reception. This can feel a bit like the end of the Royal Variety Performance if you are not careful and don't keep it moving briskly, but it is an essential part of the hospitality.

The order is thus: bride's mother, bride's father, groom's mother, groom's father, bride, groom.

A booming toastmaster or master of ceremonies should announce the guests as they approach the front of the queue. Guests should keep conversation very brief or else the newly-weds might well be divorced by the time it is over.

Do say 'You look so radiant/handsome. Let's have more of a chat later.'

Don't say 'How are you feeling? You look exhausted. Go careful on the booze.'

TOP TABLE

Aristos and wannabe aristos love a seating plan (which, remember, you should call *place à table*). Wedding receptions are no exception and the top table has a protocol to follow. From spectators' left to right: chief bridesmaid, father of the groom, mother of the bride, groom, bride, father of the bride, mother of the groom, best man.

If you are one of those to be seated on the top table, you should play down your elevated position and adopt the attitude that it's a bit of a bore having to sit there but duty is duty. This is essential advice for everyone, whether you are the chief bridesmaid or the groom.

Do say 'I'd much rather sit with everyone else, but custom is custom.'

Don't say 'Shame you weren't deemed important enough to join us on the top table.'

SPEECHES AND TOASTS

Even sophisticated weddings have interminable speeches, especially by the best man who will frequently deliver a self-indulgent, rambling address, which he and about two others will find hilarious, while everybody else looks politely on.

The best best man's speeches will be five-or-so minutes in length, paint an amusing yet reflective vignette of the groom and contain jokes that won't offend anyone. Very few achieve this feat, sadly. The lesson here is that you should choose your best man wisely. He will be the most public of all your friends on the day and can speak volumes about your social standing (past or future). The last thing you want is a self-appointed wit flirting dangerously with bad taste, as in: 'Having lived with each other for some time, the bride and groom's wedding night will be less of a voyage of discovery and more of a trip down memory lane.'

The correct procedure for speeches and toasts at British weddings is as follows:

First speech

Who Father of the bride (or whoever gave the bride away)
Purpose To enthuse about the bride, then enthuse about the groom (however much he doesn't like him)
Tone Affectionate and complimentary, stressing how fortunate the groom is
Toast To the bride and groom

Second speech

Who The groom
Purpose To thank everybody for coming, gush about new wife, brown-nose to new parents-in-law for raising such a lovely daughter and for hosting a wonderful reception (assuming they have done), thank guests for their generous presents (even though they're still wrapped)

Tone Modest, respectful, grateful, amazed at good fortune
Toast To the bridesmaids (avoiding the temptation to sound lecherous)

Third speech

Who The best man
Purpose To provide an amusing and entertaining portrait of the groom
Tone Warm, funny, slightly irreverent and definitely not smutty or tasteless (*see* above)
Toast Traditionally, there is no toast here, but a second toast to the happy couple has crept into fashion.

WEDDING CAKE

The *pièce de résistance* of the wedding breakfast is the cake. It is important to know that no one of good breeding has bride and groom figurines on top.

'Thank you, Rector. It was a lovely funeral.
We must have one again some time.'

Audrey fforbes-Hamilton
To the Manor Born

ETIQUETTE WHEN DISPATCHED

DEATH NOTICES

A death notice should simply state the facts. Sentimentality and gushing tributes are not the done thing.

A correct notice should read:

PARKER – On 4th May, Ruth Iona.

However, you can also include a little bit of factual information, such as key relatives and the time and place of the funeral:

PARKER – On 4th May at home. Ruth Iona, beloved wife of Michael. Funeral service at St Mark's Church, Church Road, Bristol, Wednesday 15th May at 11am. Private family committal afterwards.

It was once practice to include the deceased's address, but common sense has stopped this as, inevitably, enterprising thieves were scouring the newspapers for ideas for their next burglary. What is important now is to give enough information that readers who may have known the deceased can identify their friends and family.

In Britain it is still thought that the smartest people die in *The Times* or *The Daily Telegraph*. However, in today's society the death notice should be placed in the newspaper that is read by the majority of the deceased's peers. For example, if the deceased was a notable figure locally, then an announcement in the local newspaper is wise – especially as national newspapers charge an extortionate and distasteful amount for such notices.

An obituary is at the discretion of a newspaper editor. They cannot be bought, unlike the above death notices, and usually only appear if the deceased has achieved some prominence during their lifetime. The best obituaries are mini-biographies that present the facts of the life just lost.

Finally, remember that a person is not socially dead until the funeral has happened. That is when they become 'the late X'. So if you are in line to inherit a title, you do not become the Earl of Irthlingborough until the organ has stopped playing at the end of the funeral.

LETTERS OF CONDOLENCE

The contents of the letter must come from the heart. Phony sentiment will stand out. Remember, however, that letters of condolence are mainly to comfort the bereaved. Say one or two positive things about the deceased but the rest should be directed at the recipient. If you make an offer of help (e.g., 'Please let us know if there's anything we can do'), then make sure you mean it.

Such letters, which should ideally be written on social correspondence paper (Basildon Bond, plain white, watermarked, will be fine), are also a good means of saying whether you will be at the funeral. If you cannot attend then, just as with responses to everyday invitations, you do not need to state why you cannot attend.

Black-edged writing paper was traditional stationery for houses in mourning but is rarely seen these days. That is not to say it is unacceptable if you happen to have any.

Although in the relatively recent past, to send an 'In Sympathy' condolence card would have been tantamount to poor taste, their use is now much more widespread. They can be useful if you did not know the deceased very well but wish to show your sympathy to your grieving friend. Yet making the effort to write a letter, rather than buying a card, is the right thing to do. If you are to really make the grade, you should follow suit.

Do not write such a letter if the death notice has instructed that the next of kin is not receiving letters at this time.

An example condolence letter is thus:

Dear Michael

It was with great sadness that I learned of Ruth's death. She was such a warm and caring woman and I know that her friends and family will miss her deeply. I remember her kindness to my mother after her operation many years ago.

Although there is little that can be said and done to ease your pain, if there is anything George or I can do to help, please do not hesitate to ask us.

Yours with very best wishes and much love,
Mary

A letter of condolence is just that – not an email or, heaven forfend, a tweet.

FUNERALS AND MEMORIALS

DRESS

Black! Black is universally the colour for funerals for principal mourners and guests alike. Anyone not in black should be treated as somewhat dubious, unless it's a memorial where you can wear anything you want (within obvious limits).

The days in which ladies religiously observed the protocol of wearing mourning dress (where they would wear outfits first in all black, then sequentially adding grey, lavender, purple, black with white) are completely gone. Black armbands have also passed from social custom and now are only really seen on football pitches. And you really don't want to be confused with a professional footballer.

Lounge suits with black tie are permissible for most funerals. Only state or ceremonial funerals – or those of a society *grandee* – require morning dress. Don't confuse morning dress with mourning dress. The U is the difference. Ironic, really, as only the 'U' would get the difference.

Female mourners, be aware that you really should wear (or carry) gloves to smart funerals. This is one of the signs of a true lady. Should you forget, try to drop into conversation how cold your hands are since you accidentally left your gloves at home. This may help to plaster over the faltering cracks of your social ascension.

Some brave and cheery souls request that mourners at a funeral should not wear black but instead turn up in jolly colours. If this is the case, then you should do as asked – within reason. An Hawaiian shirt is not really appropriate. Wear a colourful tie or scarf under a casual jacket – if you must.

FLOWERS

In nearly every culture, flowers are associated with death. But remember that they are not intended to comfort the living but to pay tribute to the dead. Therefore, one does not write 'In deepest sympathy' on the card, but 'In loving memory' or 'My dear friend Henry'. The envelope should be addressed to the deceased, also.

While flowers are a must at funerals, word wreaths are a must not. Even in death, people are judging social class as, unlike we humans, class is eternal. Big wreaths with 'Nan' spelled out in daffodils are best avoided. If anyone suggests such a thing, quickly nip it in the bud, citing that it's not what she would have wanted. Indeed, say that she had once intimated to you that she thought such tributes rather 'tacky' and found traditional floral arrangements much more to her liking. Nan would thank you for it.

GRIEVING

The upper classes take a stoic attitude when it comes to either their own death or other people's. The general consensus is that it's a bit of a bore having to die. When anyone dies, the aristocracy tries not to show any overt signs of emotion. Dissolving in a flood of tears is never the done thing. If you wish to cry, then make sure to do it in private, away from others to minimise awkwardness. Public shows of grief are just not done.

CHURCH ETIQUETTE

Even in times of great sadness, etiquette matters. The first 'set piece' of the service is the procession of principal mourners. The vicar or whoever is conducting the service usually leads the procession, followed by the coffin/pall-bearers and then the family.

In the instance of the deceased being a married man, the procession would be as follows:

Coffin
Widow and eldest son
Other children of deceased
Deceased's parents
Siblings of deceased

The same is applicable for a widower, with the obvious change.

Where there is no surviving spouse, then the children walk in single file in order of age (the eldest being at the front). In more modern times, the children can walk together in pairs, side by side or with their respective partners.

As the coffin enters, the congregation is expected to stand. The congregation and principal mourners are invited to sit down by the priest.

As previously mentioned, the uppers love a seating plan, and at a funeral there is a placement code to be respected, too. Correctly, the principal mourners will sit at the front-right of the church (as you look up the nave towards the altar). The priest should have these seats reserved for the chief mourners, as many are not aware of this rule.

Should any members of the Royal Family be in attendance, they will sit in the front-left pews. Bluffers should always leave the front row free 'just in case' royalty puts in an appearance.

During the service, usual church manners apply. Stand to sing all hymns and other songs that you may be asked to participate in; kneel or bow for prayers and psalms. Regardless of your religious viewpoint, you should be aware that not following (or knowing) how to behave in the house of God is a sure-fire way to precipitate your own funeral in high society.

At the end of the service, the principal mourners usually follow the coffin out. If there is no coffin to follow (in other words, at a memorial service), then they would just walk out first, and other guests can then follow.

If the principals feel up to it, an informal line-up outside the church can be organised. The order is the same as the procession – the chief principal mourner greets guests first, followed by the eldest son, and so on.

SAYING THE RIGHT THING

When you speak directly to the grieving party, try to avoid saying the wrong thing. Death can be an awkward subject for many and can lead to some toe-curlingly awful moments.

Avoid the 'Dirty Dozen' following phrases:

'He's in a better place.'
'He didn't deserve to go.'
'It's God's will.'
'There's never a right time.'
'At least it was painless.'
'He wouldn't want you to grieve.'
'He had a good innings.'
'It must have come as something of a relief.'
'I know how you feel.'
'Has he left you comfortable?'
'I don't suppose his MCC blazer is going spare, is it?'
'He would have enjoyed the send-off.'

Instead, stick to simple phrases such as:

'I'm so sorry.'
'She was an extraordinary person.'
'Please know that Mary and I are thinking of you.'
'We will all miss her so much.'

Also note that the traditionalists prefer the 'call a spade a spade' approach to talking about death. Phrases such as 'when Peter passed away' should be avoided. Instead, say 'when Peter died'. Talking of 'your loss' is also a pitfall. Your patrician mourner is more than likely to turn and say, 'I haven't lost Mark. He died.'

Remember:

Do say 'Your father was an example to us all.'

Don't say 'Has he left you enough to retire on?'

WAKES

Perversely, a wake is often one of the more enjoyable social gatherings as the tension of the funeral or memorial has passed and old friends and family reacquaint themselves over a drink. Certainly in Britain, the humour reflex begins to kick in. Yet you must not admit to this.

Historically termed 'funeral breakfast', a wake is the gathering (usually a meal) that happens immediately after a funeral. They used to be lavish affairs, but today they are usually simple buffets held in the family home or at an hotel.

If there is to be a wake then the vicar will usually announce the details towards the end of the service. It may also be printed at the back of the service sheet with wording along the lines of, 'The family wish to welcome you all to The Grange at 1 o'clock for a buffet lunch'. More often than not these can turn into an enjoyable celebration of the dear departed's 'best moments'. After all, it's what he/she would have wanted.

'There is a forgotten, nay almost forbidden word, which means more to me than any other. That word is England.'

Sir Winston Churchill

FILLIES, FLOWERS AND FLOTILLAS (THE SEASON)

I n the dreamy Edwardian days of *Downton Abbey*, The Season was April to July and was when suitable young ladies would be trotted out at key social events, such as the Chelsea Flower Show or Royal Ascot, in order to catch the eye of a suitable young man, with the view to marriage. If a girl failed to catch anyone's eye after one season of 'coming out', she could have a go the next year, although anything after two seasons was a disaster and really only the fate of the plain (i.e., Lady Edith Crawley). They would remain unmarried and probably have a thankless career as a governess.

When the Queen stopped the ritual of young ladies (debutantes – but refer to them as 'debs' when referencing 'coming out' in conversation) being presented at court in 1958, The Season began to die a death, although the set-piece events still survive. And such events can be a good place for those looking to marry well. Note that in any conversation about The Season, it is only ever referred to as such – never the British or English season, even though it takes place exclusively in England.

THE BOAT RACE

This is a minor event in The Season, but to many it is a very important minor event. The two universities collectively known as 'Oxbridge' go head to head in March or April in a four-and-a-quarter mile race down the Thames.

The bluffer should not be alarmed when asked whether they support the Darks or the Lights. This is not a form of racism but simply nicknames for Oxford and Cambridge. Entry-level bluffing is to know that Oxford is the Darks and Cambridge the Lights. As to which team you support, quickly calculate how many more friends you have who went to one as opposed to the other. And if you went to either of the universities then, obviously, support your alma mater.

As a spectator, you could slip into conversation that it is such a shame that they let postgraduate non-Brits join the teams, as it takes the Corinthian spirit out of it all. Excessively muscled Americans and Australians are now regularly found among the eight oarsmen (not 'rowers') and it would not be unfair to state that they are chosen for their muscle. All crew are chosen for their muscle.

On top of the eight oarsmen, each boat has one cox, which is either a small man or a petite woman. Novices will make the obvious 'cox' jokes (e.g., *Private Eye*'s famous 'Colemanballs': 'Despite their diminutive cox, the Cambridge crew is surging to victory.'). These are to be avoided, and if you hear anyone trying to tell one, disassociate yourself from them immediately. They will not be present next year.

The event is usually followed by a Boat Race Ball in the evening.

RHS CHELSEA FLOWER SHOW

More commonly referred to as just 'Chelsea', this is the first of The Season's biggies and it always takes place in the third week of May.

Dress is summery; women will wear lightweight fabrics, and they will always be cold.

Do say 'I'm particularly interested in viewing the peonies.'

Don't say 'I do hope we see that nice Alan Titchmarsh.'

Chelsea is split over five days. The first three are the ones on which you want to be seen in attendance. Monday is the royal preview, followed by the charity gala evening. Tuesday and Wednesday are for Royal Horticultural Society members (it is strongly suggested that bluffers should apply for membership of this society, as not only will you get access to tickets but you can use the car sticker to lend a touch of class to your car). The final two days are for that ignominious section of society: the general public (usually referred to dismissively by uppers as simply 'the general').

Note that the grand marquee at the hub of the great event operates a one-way system. It may be frustrating to have to queue to gain admission but you ignore it at your social peril. While queuing, you could mention how you remember your grandmother telling you that when she used to go as a child the flower show was at Temple Gardens on the Embankment. This will show that your family has always been coming to Chelsea and you will score maximum bluffing points.

GLYNDEBOURNE FESTIVAL OPERA

The only summer festival beginning with G that smart people go to is Glyndebourne. Glastonbury is a 'rock' festival held somewhere in the West Country and is best avoided by etiquette bluffers who, if asked why, might venture that there's not enough room to unfurl a picnic rug and erect a parasol.

Glyndebourne is an opera festival that runs from May to August in East Sussex in the grounds of the 600-year-old house of the same name.* Although it is a key part of The Season, organisers and performers tend not to like being labelled as such, so it's best not to say anything about the subject when in attendance.

Dress is still evening dress (black tie), although experienced Glyndebourne-goers will know to bring extra layers for when it gets a bit chilly.

ROYAL ASCOT

This is the peak of the social season. Although you will of course know that Ascot holds 26 days of racing a year, it is only the five-day meeting in June that is termed 'Royal Ascot'.

Whatever you do, don't call it 'horse racing'. It is just 'racing' – as the attitude of the upper classes is what on earth else do you race?

*See The Bluffer's Guide to Opera.

It is probably a good idea to stay at home if you are not allowed admission to the Royal Enclosure. This is the invitation-only area of the racecourse where only the cream of society will be found. You have to be proposed for membership by someone who is already a member and has been for four years. Not everyone is allowed entrance, and applications are reviewed on a case-by-case basis. Until 1955, divorcees were not permitted, and still to this day anyone with a criminal record or who is an undischarged bankrupt is barred.

Don't call it 'horse racing'. It is just 'racing' – as the attitude of the upper classes is what on earth else do you race?

Tuesday is the first racing day and is very popular. Wednesday is the bookmakers' favourite when more betting takes place than on any other day. Thursday is Ladies' Day, although this is a misnomer as men are also allowed entry. Friday and Saturday are less busy and quite popular with younger racegoers.

Before the racing begins, the royal party arrives through the golden gates of Windsor Great Park in open carriages, drawn by Windsor Greys. (NB: Windsor Greys are a type of horse, not senior members of the Royal Family.) The carriages will sweep their passengers directly into the heart of the action; you will not have that advantage and will have to consider the irksome matter of parking.

There is a certain amount of debate as to what the best car park is at Royal Ascot. Number 1 Car Park is probably the best, and most certainly the smartest place for your luxury picnic from Fortnum's (Harrods will do at a pinch, but certainly not anything from a chain – even if it is Waitrose). Number 7 Car Park is reserved for Royal Enclosure members only, so this is a socially acceptable car park as well.

Dress for the Royal Enclosure is morning dress, which (remember) is not to be termed 'morning suit'. Referring to it as such will immediately expose you as a bluffer. Your Royal Enclosure status will probably be withdrawn – quicker than you can say 'Coach Park Number 11'.

Royal Ascot is synonymous with hats: top hats for the men and often elaborate hats for the women. The rules have changed in the last two years, and those awful 'fascinators' are no longer allowed. There was never anything fascinating about fascinators, and the dress code for Ascot has finally realised this. You should adopt the same attitude when asked about such things. No real lady will ever have worn one or even contemplated wearing such a thing. (NB: You might still see people in fascinators at Royal Ascot, but they will just be Grandstand people, not Royal Enclosure.)

Also not to be worn by or seen on women are spaghetti straps, halter necks, off-the-shoulder outfits or exposed midriffs. This would rather restrict the cast of *The Only Way is Essex*. And that is exactly the point.

Do say 'Thank heavens they've tightened the dress code!'

Don't say 'I could really cheer this place up a bit with a boob tube.'

Ladies must be aware that while they may wish to show off a marvellous hat, they need to be able to wear it continuously, as ladies' hats are not to be removed throughout the meeting. A large cartwheel on their head is likely to be unsuitable as it will likely be both cumbersome and very uncomfortable. Hatpins should be used to hold the hat in place.

Cravats really stand out as the wrong choice for men at Royal Ascot; correct etiquette requires a normal necktie with morning dress. For men attending Ladies' Day, the morning coat and top hat should normally be light grey, rather than the customary black.

When among racing types, talk about 'The Going'. This is the description of the ground conditions experienced by the horse. Knowledge of this more technical aspect of racing will do your credibility no harm at all. The Going scale is: heavy, soft, good to soft, good, good to firm, firm and hard. The Going is announced around seven days before the meeting. If the course is too hard, then the clerk of the course will take appropriate measures with his watering can.

HENLEY ROYAL REGATTA

Henley is a rowing event which takes place in the Oxfordshire town of Henley-on-Thames for five days in early July. Strictly, it is called Henley Royal Regatta – but you will never hear it referred to as that. If you do, keep an eye on the perpetrator. He or she could be a bluffer, and there's nothing more dangerous than a bluffer with a flimsy grasp of the lingo giving the game away.

The reigning monarch is the patron and always has been, although Henley is not an event regularly attended by the Royal Family, which has never shown much interest in rowing. Royal-watchers should stick to Ascot.

Even though you will be attending Henley to reaffirm your social position, knowing a few facts about the event and the rowing side of things will help. You should know, for example, that Henley, although endorsed by British Rowing and the International Rowing Federation, has its own rules, as it predates both of the sport's governing bodies. You should also be aware that the course is slightly longer than the sport's standards, at one mile and 550 yards (roughly 2,112 metres). The most prestigious race is the Grand Challenge Cup for eights. This is the one you should affect to have the most interest in watching.

Henley applies a strict dress code in the Stewards' Enclosure. Men must wear a tie, either with a suit or with a blazer and smart trousers. As a general rule, boating blazers must only be worn if you have been part of a boating team at some point (especially if you were a Dark or a Light). Many clothing designers will stock boating blazer look-a-likes with crests on the outer top pocket to make them look 'authentic'. These should be avoided like the plague.

Women must wear skirts below the knee, with no splits

or divides. Trousers on ladies are also not allowed.

The Ascot Royal Enclosure equivalent is the Stewards' Enclosure, where membership is limited to 6,500. To gain entry, you have to be proposed and seconded by existing members, and then wait for donkey's years until you are (maybe) accepted. Even celebrated former rowers, whose application will be fast-tracked, still have to wait for a few years to gain entry. Any bluffer who manages to get into this enclosure as a proper member has effectively won a gold medal in the bluffing stakes and should be commended.

WIMBLEDON

The Championships at Wimbledon, which takes place the last week of June and first week of July, is the world's oldest tennis tournament, the only major one played on grass and, according to those who organise it, the most prestigious. It is really only for serious tennis fans and there isn't much social credibility attached to it. It is not an event to attend just to be seen, sadly.

The stereotypical image of Wimbledon is, of course, strawberries and cream. Eating them is still optional. But thousands of pounds of strawberries will be consumed during the fortnight. It's a tradition which started back in 1953 when they first allowed a strawberry vendor onto the site. And then sometime in the early 1970s they started dunking them in cream. And like Pimms at Henley, Wimbledon took possession of the idea. You, as a bluffer, should never be seen eating them – not that you should denigrate the prospect. The best thing to say is simply:

'Over the years I've become a little inured to their appeal', and then head in the direction of the Champagne tent.

If you happen to find yourself on the most famous lawns since Versailles (*see* page 5), a useful tip is to eschew Centre Court for Court Three, which has a fearsome reputation as the 'Graveyard of Champions', and a place where you might actually witness a thrilling contest.

> **Do say** 'The game of lawn tennis was actually invented in Birmingham, England, in 1865 by Harry Gem and Juan Bautista Augurio Perera.'*

> **Don't say** 'Wahey! I can see her pants from here.'

OTHER RUNNERS AND RIDERS

You should also be aware of the principal contenders on the waiting list for inclusion in The Season's more established events. They include the Cheltenham Festival (say, 'Great fun, but not really the place to be seen'), Glorious Goodwood ('No royalty so no point'), Cowes Week ('Lots of boats if you like that sort of thing'), Goodwood Festival of Speed and Goodwood Revival Meeting ('Lots of old cars if you like that sort of thing') and Veuve Clicquot Gold Cup Polo ('An outside chance that one or both of the Waleses will be there, so always worth a punt').

*See *The Bluffer's Guide to Tennis.*

CORGI COURTESY
(A ROYAL AUDIENCE)

Those who have followed the instructions in this book to the letter may very well find themselves mingling with royalty at some stage. Of course, there's no saying what sort of royalty. One-hundred per cent retention of advice and information will mean you can hope for the British Royal Family. Anything less than 70% observance will mean you might have to settle for a Swedish royal (in which case, it is suggested that you hide the good china and bring out the Ikea stuff).

But let's assume that you have taken this guide's advice seriously and, as a result, you are now hovering on the fringes of British royal circles.

When meeting any member of the Royal Family, you will be expected to bow or curtsey. Men bow from the neck. Bowing from the waist, if you don't know what you're doing, may well result in you 'headbutting' an unsuspecting royal who might be stepping forward to confide something amusing. So take care. Women curtsey by placing one foot behind the other and just gently bobbing. Don't go down too far or else you may never come back up. Women can opt to bow instead of the traditional curtsey, though it would be the unconventional choice so is not recommended.

Anyone with republican tendencies will probably not be in the position of courting royalty; they'll be too busy manning the barricades or stoking the braziers outside one of the royal palaces. But mention the possibility of a 'gong' and things have a tendency to change very quickly. Veteran Labour politicians with a chance of a peerage are prone to trot out the old cliché: 'I bow to no man but I'll make an exception in the case of Her Majesty.'

When discussing the etiquette involved in bowing to royalty, you will not take offence when someone of a republican persuasion insists that it is a shameful and unconscionable show of obeisance. Listen to them, smile politely and say, 'How lovely'. Entering into an argument is fruitless and even the Royal Family will not stoop to argue their case. Republican types are best ignored.

If you happen to be a citizen of a country where the British Royal Family is not your monarchy, then that is your misfortune. But be aware that although strictly you do not have to bow, scrape or curtsey, it can seem churlish not to. Former Australian prime minister, Julia Gillard, failed to do anything except stand there gawping when meeting the Queen on the latter's visit in 2011, and former prime minister's wife Cherie Blair was infamous for her reluctance to curtsey. The Queen was not noticeably fazed by any of this, and neither should you be if you notice anyone else petulantly refusing. Simply make a mental note to strike them off your dinner party list. They'll probably have their suit jacket fastened incorrectly or be showing too much cleavage anyway.

When meeting the Queen, she must be addressed as 'Your Majesty', followed by 'Ma'am'. All other members of 'The Firm' are addressed 'Your Royal Highness', followed by 'Sir' or 'Ma'am'. The exception is Princess Michael of Kent, who has a boy's name, and can thus be addressed as either.

Do not extend your hand to members of royalty; let them extend their hand to you. Don't take it personally if no hand is proffered. They shake hundreds of hands a day and can't greet everyone personally – although if you are courting the friendship of one of their relatives, this probably isn't a good sign for the future. It might be because you've said pardon or worn brown shoes on a Thursday at Clarence House. You'll only have yourself to blame.

If you are having tea (never 'taking tea', remember), wait to be seated until the Queen, or any female royalty, have sat down first – regardless of your own sex. Tea in the royal household is at 5 o'clock, rather than 4 o'clock like in many other houses. Do not ask why or make remarks that you're hungry as you've had to wait so long for this, or you'll be evicted quicker than you can say 'Paul Burrell'. (As it happens, tea is served later for the simple reason that they prefer it – as their dinner is later than most, at 8.15pm.)

Any dialogue with royalty requires that you gracefully allow them to steer the topics and direction of conversation. Asking direct questions used to be frowned on, but today the rules are slightly more relaxed. Yet it is not good practice to ask anything too personal. Broadcaster John Humphrys made two errors when recently meeting Her Majesty at the official opening of BBC Broadcasting House: he asked her a direct, personal question about the Duke of Edinburgh's health – while his arms were folded. No chance of a knighthood there in the foreseeable future, then.

Do say 'Did Your Majesty enjoy lunch?'

Don't say 'What did the corgis have for lunch today?'

If you refer to a member of the Royal Family in conversation, then use either their title or honorific:

'The Earl of Wessex was particularly interested in the zumba class.'

or

'I told His Royal Highness he could join in later.'

Avoid using the pronoun 'you'. Opt instead for 'Your Majesty' or 'Your Royal Highness':

'Would Your Majesty like to view the interfaith, multi-use skate park now?'

Avoid referring to the Royal Family as 'The Royals': it's just a bit common and sounds like a sitcom.

ROYAL INVITATIONS

If you have managed to befriend a member of royalty, your new social position may come with invitations to events at one of the royal palaces.

Invitations from the Queen are not really 'invitations'. They are commands. Unless you have exceptional mitigating circumstances, such as being dead or close to death, they are not declined. In almost all circumstances, guests will be contacted by telephone well in advance to warn them of the date, so invitations are never turned down.

As with normal invitations, you should reply in the third person and replies should be handwritten and sent back within a couple of days.

A reply should read something like:

Mr John Humphrys presents his compliments to the Lord Chamberlain and has the honour to obey Her Majesty's command to attend a luncheon at Buckingham Palace on Friday, 14th May at 1 o'clock.

(Like that's going to happen.)

GARDEN PARTIES

Perhaps one of the best known of royal functions is the garden party.

Four garden parties take place each year: three at Buckingham Palace and one at the Palace of Holyroodhouse in Edinburgh. These parties are given to reward and acknowledge those who have made significant contributions to their communities or worthy causes (i.e., charitable volunteers, teachers, doctors and nurses). Yet there will also be members from the diplomatic corps and selected guests of the Royal Family, who might include you.

Although the gates of Buckingham Palace open at 3pm, the Queen and Duke of Edinburgh arrive at 4pm on the West Terrace, and when they reach the steps down into the gardens, the National Anthem plays and everyone stands very still. Resist the urge to sing the anthem. You are not a football player (not that they can remember the words, anyway). The anthem also plays at 6pm to mark the end of the event – a terribly smart way to get rid of your guests, although (sadly) this tactic should not be deployed at your own events.

♔

Rushing to the tent
upon arrival and piling up a plate
is not the done thing.

What is thought to be the world's longest tea tent (400 feet long) is erected down one side of the grounds at Buckingham Palace to serve guests finger sandwiches, tea, scones and pastries. Rushing to the tent upon arrival and piling up a plate is not the done thing. The correct approach is to amble casually to the tent, acting as if you attend every garden party.

Her Majesty has her own private enclosure at her garden parties where dignitaries and politicians are entertained. If you have the good fortune to be invited in, don't take out your mobile phone and start taking pictures. You will find yourself quickly escorted away.

Guests have the unique opportunity to relax and explore the gardens, which are normally shut to the general public. Yet if you get asked (by a normal guest) whether you want to tour the gardens, you should say with a slight sigh, 'Well, all right, although I have seen them many times before.'

PRECEDENCE AND SUCCESSION

Before you enter royal circles, you should make sure your royal history and protocol is up to scratch. One key mistake made by many is not knowing the difference between the line of succession and the order of precedence. The latter is known only to members of the royal family (so don't ask your royal connection what it is). It is at the discretion of the Queen, and she can change it at will. She is the Queen after all. Precedence is what determines the seniority and rank of royalty at official events. The Queen is the highest-ranking woman and the Duke of Edinburgh is the highest-ranking man. Your only chance of getting on the list is to get engaged to a member of the royal family – and even then it's not certain.

The current line of succession is as follows:

1. Charles, Prince of Wales
2. Prince William, Duke of Cambridge
3. Prince George of Cambridge
4. Prince George's sibling(s), in order of birth
5. Prince Henry of Wales (better known as Prince Harry)
6. Prince Andrew, Duke of York

7. Princess Beatrice of York
8. Princess Eugenie of York
9. Prince Edward, Earl of Wessex
10. James, Viscount Severn
11. The Lady Louise Mountbatten-Windsor
12. Anne, The Princess Royal
13. Mr Peter Phillips
14. Miss Savannah Phillips
15. Miss Isla Phillips
16. Mrs Michael Tindall (Zara Phillips)

There are many more in line to the throne, but really it becomes not worth counting or worrying about after 16. The chances of them all going down with terminal botulism at the same time are relatively slim.

There's no point in pretending that you know everything about etiquette – nobody does (not even the author) – but if you've got this far and absorbed at least a modicum of the information and advice contained within these pages, then you will almost certainly know more than 99% of the rest of the human race about what etiquette is, who invented it, why we still need it and how not to breach it.

What you now do with this information is up to you, but here's a suggestion: be confident about your newfound knowledge, see how far it takes you, but above all have fun using it. You are now a bona fide expert in the art of bluffing about a code of behaviour with which you will need to be very familiar if you seek to join the upper echelons of high society. And, most importantly, remember never to say 'pardon' or 'toilet'. Especially in the same sentence.

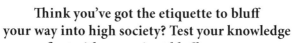

**Think you've got the etiquette to bluff
your way into high society? Test your knowledge
first with our quiz at bluffers.com.**

GLOSSARY

Baby/bridal shower You have no idea what these are but they are probably best avoided.

Bottom button (of a suit jacket or waistcoat) To be frank, this should have a little dust on it, as it remains untouched and unfastened, unless you have no breeding.

Bowing to Japanese royalty The bow here is from the waist. Go down first and strive to be as parallel to the floor as possible. Never rise from the bow until they have risen from their bow (which will vary in depth depending on who you are). If you put your back out doing this, then that is the price you pay for mixing with royalty.

Coasters Bizarre little things middle-class homes have spread neatly around their surfaces for drinks.

Comme il faut Nicer way of saying 'as it should be', or correct behaviour.

De rigueur Probably one of the most important expressions in the society lexicon, this means 'as required by etiquette'.

Droit du seigneur This sounds like it might have something to do with etiquette, but it's a somewhat outmoded concept these days, referring to the 'right of a lord' to deflower a virgin on her wedding eve.

Going, The Racing term for the ground conditions. Drop it into all conversations in the Royal Enclosure at Ascot.

HKLP An acronym meaning 'Holds Knife Like a Pen'. One of the most damning indictments that can be made of a bluffer, because it will immediately identify you as somebody who hasn't been tutored in the finer points of dining etiquette. If you are caught doing it by mistake, there is only one way that you can bluff your way out of the situation: immediately claim that you suffer from 'trigger finger' (medical name 'Dupuytren's contracture'), a genetic condition that causes connective tissue in the hand to pull fingers inwards. You might add that it's the only way you can hold a knife and you inherited it via the Habsburg line of the family. But even after citing this condition, you should still prepare for irrevocable social isolation.

Invite To you, it's a verb and nothing else. To those not in the know, it's a synonym for 'invitation'.

Lèse-majesté Something to be avoided at all costs; a grievous insult to your monarch. (Are you listening, Mr Humphrys?)

Money A subject never discussed with anyone, even your bank (which you'd prefer would stop calling you).

Morning suit What *parvenus* call morning dress.

Noblesse oblige The idea that if born into the upper social classes you will behave honourably to those less privileged. It's a marvellous thing in principle.

NQOCD Initialism: Not Quite Our Class, Darling.

Ordinaire Nicer way of saying 'a bit common'.

Pardon Word worse than the F-word.

Place à table Smart way of saying seating plan. Ask your hostess if there is one and win maximum bluffing points.

PLU Initialism: People Like Us.

Precedence The order of rank. This will be very important in your new life.

Service plates/chargers Coasters for dinner plates.

Social networking What you do at cocktail parties and hunt balls. Absolutely nothing to do with 'media'.

Solemn selfie Shamelessly taking a photograph of yourself (sometimes with others) on your mobile phone at memorials or funerals of great statesmen. Unlikely to become acceptable behaviour, despite the best efforts of President Obama and Prime Minister Cameron.

Toilet One of the foulest words in the English language. Blame the French.

BLUFFING NOTES

Bluffing Notes

Bluffing Notes

Bluffing Notes

MAXIMUM CREDIBILITY, MINIMUM EFFORT

A world of bluffing awaits: books,
gift sets and collections at bluffers.com

BEER	JAZZ
BOND	MANAGEMENT
CARS	OPERA
CATS	POETRY
CHOCOLATE	THE QUANTUM UNIVERSE
CRICKET	ROCK
CYCLING	RUGBY
DOGS	SEX
ETIQUETTE	SKIING
FISHING	SOCIAL MEDIA
FOOD	STAND-UP COMEDY
FOOTBALL	SURFING
GOLF	TENNIS
HIKING	UNIVERSITY
HORSERACING	WINE
INSIDER HOLLYWOOD	YOUR OWN BUSINESS

SIGN UP FOR YOUR WEEKLY
DOSE OF BLUFFING AT
BLUFFERS.COM

@BLUFFERSGUIDE

7012467R00080

Printed in Germany
by Amazon Distribution
GmbH, Leipzig